Travellers' Last Rights

Responding to Death in a Cultural Context

Compiled by
Jacinta Brack and Stephen Monaghan

Edited by Jacinta Brack

Published by the Parish of the Travelling People

St Laurence House

6 New Cabra Road

Phibsborough

Dublin 7

Tel: 01 8388 874

Fax: 01 8388 901

Email: mail@ptrav.ie

ISBN 0-9521120-1-9

Design and production:

Type IT, Northside Business Centre, East Wall Road, Dublin 3

Printed by ColourBooks Ltd, Baldoyle, Dublin 13

CONTENTS

ACKNOWLEDGEMENTS

Acknowledgement and warm thanks are extended to those who co-operated in the development of this publication, including Travellers and service providers working in health, social work, pastoral and clerical ministry, chaplaincy, funeral undertaking and policing.

We are grateful also to individual Travellers who shared their personal experiences.

Thanks are extended to the staff of the Parish of the Travelling People, Des Byrne of Behaviour & Attitudes Market Research for his generous expertise and in compiling the data in chapter 6, Christy Kenneally, Fr John Gallagher, Michael and Mary Hutchinson, Nova Farris of the Health Service Executive, the Traveller Health Unit, the Dublin City Coroners Office, Alan O'Reilly and Pat Conneely of Typeform Repro, and Antoinette Walker.

This book is dedicated to the Traveller community and to the memory of their deceased loved ones.

OVERVIEW

This book explores issues related to death in a cultural context specific to Travellers. As a backdrop the book draws on two distinct areas of research: one presenting mortality findings from a sample of Traveller deaths during a 10-year period in the Dublin area; and the other presenting outcomes from qualitative research undertaken among Travellers and service providers, which was based on factors affecting the delivery and uptake of services specific to times of death and bereavement.

It is intended that the information compiled will help improve contact between Travellers and service providers, for example, hospital staff, clergy, Gardaí, prison chaplains and funeral undertakers during times of illness and death. It is also hoped that the Traveller mortality findings will assist those advocating culturally appropriate services for Travellers and will contribute to the knowledge base required to implement public health and prevention strategies on some of the issues raised.

FORMAT

The first section presents some background information specific to Travellers and reflects on death as a cross-cultural experience. Following that two personal accounts are presented: one a Traveller family's perspective of bereavement, the other a minister providing a pastoral service to Travellers in the context of death.

Section 2 provides a study of Traveller mortality compiled by the Parish of the Travelling People. Those deaths were recorded following requests for a sacramental service from Traveller parioshiers living in the Dublin diocese, over a 10-year period.

Section 3 presents a series of recommendations specific to the area of each service provider, developed from issues raised at focus groups and through other consultative processes undertaken with Travellers and service providers.

Section 4 presents two research reports from focus groups conducted by Behaviour & Attitudes Market Research on behalf of the Parish of the Travelling People. These reports related the experiences of Travellers, and service providers in contact with Travellers, at times of death, and identified issues related to barriers to delivering the type of service appropriate to Travellers' needs.

CONTENT AND FINDINGS

Information contained in this book is informed by three key sources:

- Qualitative research commissioned by the Parish of the Travelling People and compiled on their behalf by Behaviour & Attitudes Market Research. It sought to establish the level of contact and experience of that contact between Travellers and relevant service provider groups at times of illness and death. Research focus groups included:

- ➢ Travellers
- ➢ Priests
- ➢ Hospital and prison chaplains
- ➢ Hospital nursing practice development co-ordinator and public health nurses.
- ➢ Social workers
- ➢ Undertaker
- ➢ Gardaí.

- A mortality study compiled from records maintained by the Parish of the Travelling People based on Traveller deaths responded to in the Dublin area from 1995 to 2004.

- Additional information was resourced from priests, parish sisters and other staff of the Parish of the Travelling People working to support the pastoral needs of Travellers.

THE ROLE OF THE PARISH

The Parish of the Travelling People was established in 1980 under the direction of the Vincentian Community in Ireland in answer to a request by the then Archbishop of Dublin to respond to the pastoral needs of Travellers throughout the diocese.

Those needs were expressed by Travellers as a result of their experience of exclusion. This prompted the Parish of the Travelling People to work in solidarity with them to have their rights realised, facilitating their equal participation within the Church and society.

A significant aspect of that work to date has been the pastoral administration of services to Travellers at times of life transition, including occasions of birth, illness and death, and in the celebration of the Catholic sacraments of christenings, communions, confirmations, weddings and funerals.

FOREWORD

We have never had it so good. Diseases that once crippled our quality of life have been consigned to medical history. Infant death is now blessedly rare and most of us can expect a ripe old age. Added to this, the emigrant ship has reversed into dry-dock; we are now a first-world country, the aspiration of immigrants from around the world. Our media constantly discuss how we respond to these new arrivals and their cultures. And yet, we seem to have turned a blind and often baleful eye at a minority culture within our own.

Travellers are citizens of our Republic. They are our own people, and, like members of the settled community, they live, die and are grieved. But, the similarities stop there. Travellers die younger and their bereaved do not enjoy the same ease of access to support services.

I welcome this publication; it is particularly timely. It's neither a rant nor a panacea but a detailed and measured outline of how a nomadic people can be marginalised within a culture like our own, and how their own culture is in danger of being subsumed by ours.

It is also a voice for the unheard and a challenge to those who have the courage to hear and act.

I wholeheartedly recommend it to all who are entrusted with providing culturally appropriate services to Travellers, particularly at times of illness, death and bereavement.

Christy Kenneally
March 2007

SECTION 1

DEATH IN A CULTURAL CONTEXT

Death is a universal experience of humankind because of its basic part in human biology and psychology. Death has an impact on people in all societies. We can assume that all societies mark the fact of a death by special events, that all societies have ways to dispose of dead bodies, and that all societies have ways to continue with life. But beyond those universals there is immense variability.

Mary Dombeck

Chapter 1
The Cross-Cultural Experience

While we share in the universal experience of death, individual cultures construct their own rites and ways of marking death significant to them. From country to country and indeed within countries differences prevail among groups. In Ireland that diversity of expression may not appear obvious, but for minority cultures like Travellers there are well-defined yet subtle differences of importance, including those linked to both symbolism and practices around death and dying.

In their book, *Rites of Death and Dying*, Boadt, Dombeck and Rutherford explore death from the perspective of cross-cultural rites and rituals and the challenges faced by minority cultures in conforming to the norms of the majority population.[1] Through the work at the Parish of the Travelling People, we have witnessed where diversity of expression can be perceived as something inferior and where Travellers as a minority are often expected to conform to majority norms. Specifically, we observe problems arising when service providers are confronted by a minority group who do not conform to majority norms and, by their difference, present challenges. Likewise, mourners often feel dispossessed if service providers, be they medical personnel, ministers, funeral directors or others, refuse to acknowledge and/or incorporate things of cultural value to them into their mourning rituals.

As Ireland's growth of new cultures continues, we are all challenged to appreciate the diversity of expression attached to many life-important events carried over and practised from other countries. And so respecting death and mourning rituals and recognising their value in many situations – for example, at hospitals, mortuaries, funeral homes, churches and cemeteries – to those bereaved is ever more important.

CULTURAL VARIABLES

In *Rites of Death and Dying*, the authors describe a particular conflict which many people from different cultural backgrounds experience when integrating into the majority population, namely, that of wishing to be seen to conform and yet having a deep-seated cultural need to mourn their dead in a particular way. While as service providers we can

---

1. Lawrence Boadt, Mary Dombeck and H. Richard Rutherford, *Rites of Death and Dying*. Collegeville: Liturgical Press, 1988.

humanly identify with a common sense of loss, we may not always grasp what the authors describe as the 'cultural variables', as these variables are often subtle and difficult to define. Working with Travellers at times of death and bereavement, we have have a good sense of – rather than a true understanding of – what is happening at those times. We are conscious of the importance of responding to specific needs to avoid denigrating things that happen as unimportant, just because we do not understand them. In Ireland people from different cultural backgrounds often have little choice but to engage with the funeral services offered and thus little opportunity to incorporate specific elements of cultural value into those services.

Boadt, Dombeck and Rutherford observe practices in the United States and note that culturally diverse expressions of grief and mourning can very quickly be lost to the general practices of the majority population: 'Moreover, the United States has continued to receive immigrants from different societies who have brought their own customs from the old country. However, most of them after two generations begin to adopt American practices like embalming and engaging of funeral specialists at the time of death. Or, they feel the pressure to do so.'

THE CROSS-CULTURAL EXPERIENCE

The emotional language used at funeral services is also raised by Boadt, Dombeck and Rutherford, and they observe that, for example, in the United States an Irish funeral might be perceived as having 'a degree of superficial levity', while an Italian funeral might have 'a great deal of dramatics'. They believe it is crucial for those who engage with and/or carry out funeral services to have some appreciation of the emotional language of the group they are connecting with and, in particular, reference to ministers. They say:

> If the minister, lay or ordained, understands the ethnic background, it is very comforting, not only that someone understands and remembers the customs, but also the pressure to change them, which comes from within the ethnic community itself. If however the minister finds himself or herself in a community alien to his or her background, then there is an opportunity to become more sensitive. Each one of these communities deserves the perceptive scrutiny of a person who is having a cross-cultural experience. The cross-cultural experience makes the analytic anthropologist or the perceptive traveller ask: 'What makes them do or say a peculiar thing like that?', this is immediately followed by: 'What we do must seem peculiar to them; where are the universals? How can I put my own values in perspective?' It is this kind of cross-cultural dialogue which transcends ethnocentrism. When one is ethnocentric, one adopts a simplistic tour-book

approach to people in different societies. A simplistic approach attempts to interact with another society without changing one's own perspectives or one's own values ……. it results in thinking that one's own customs and beliefs are better than others.

Many Travellers have no choice but to engage with service providers who will respond to their needs but out of their own cultural context. In the year 2000, a national settled population survey carried out by the Citizen Traveller Campaign indicated that 65 per cent of Irish people 'had no contact with Travellers' and that the general pattern of contact between Travellers and settled people was 'relatively infrequent', particularly in regard to 'socialising, working together and shared school experiences'. This separation of cultures (the reasons for which are sometimes based on exclusion and discrimination) to some degree prohibits the improvement of contact between service providers and Travellers, including at times of death and mourning.

Over many years and in various areas of service provision, we have witnessed how people (Travellers) who desire something different are often defined as awkward and demanding by those who cannot grasp what is being asked for. While accepting the challenges of working outside of our own familiar practices, there is an importance to acknowledging rather than dismissing difference, and in seeking ways to incorporate those differences into the rites and rituals we take for granted.

The observations as described by the authors of *Rites of Death and Dying* should have resonance for those engaged with Travellers at times of death and mourning and furthermore challenge us as service providers to embrace the cross-cultural experience.

We hope the reflections and findings in this book will also help in that process.

Chapter 2

Travellers: A Summary

POPULATION

Travellers are a small indigenous ethnic community in Ireland, accounting for 0.6 per cent of the total national population and representing 23,700 people in the Census of 2002[2] – figures for the Census of 2006 are unavailable at time of print – though an unofficial estimate is thought to be closer to 30,000 people. While the spread of the population is widely distributed, almost 50 per cent of Travellers live in four counties: 24 per cent in Dublin, 12 per cent in Galway, 5 per cent in Limerick and 7 per cent in Cork. Outside of Ireland, approximately 15,000 Irish Travellers live in Britain and 10,000 Travellers of Irish descent live in the USA.[3]

In the 2002 Census, the composition of the population continued to reflect a high birth rate and low life expectancy with Travellers over 65 years accounting for only 3.3 per cent of the population compared with 11.1 per cent of the general population, and 2 out of every 5 Travellers were aged less than 15 years compared with 1 out of every 5 in the general population.

HEALTH STATUS

No national statistics are available specific to Traveller health and mortality. The latest data is that of the 1986 Economic, Social and Research Institute (ESRI) Report, which found that 'Traveller life expectancy is equivalent to that of settled people in Ireland in the 1940s'.[4]

In 2002, the long-awaited report *Traveller Health – A National Strategy 2002–2005* from the Department of Health and Children acknowledged this paucity of information and made recommendations to address the situation. This resulted in the formation of a Working Group on Traveller Ethics and Research in 2003 and the development of a pilot study to collect information on ethnicity from the Hospital Inpatient Enquiry and Perinatal (HIPE) Systems, which began in May 2004 at the Rotunda and Tallaght

2. National Census 2002. Central Statistics Office.
3. Travellers' Health Status Study. Dublin: Health Research Board, 1986.
4. Economic, Social and Research Institute, 1986.

Hospitals. Also a Traveller needs assessment and health status study was to be initiated and completed in 2006; however this has not been undertaken to date.

Without specific data, results from Census 2002 and all anecdotal evidence continue to support the findings of the 1987 Health Research Board Study, which found that Traveller's health is significantly worse than that of the settled community and that Travellers have higher rates for all causes of death compared to the general population. When the data was compared at that time it also concluded that settled men had a life expectancy of 75 years while Traveller men had a life expectancy of 65 years. Settled women had a life expectancy of 78 years, while Traveller women had a life expectancy of 65 years. In respect of infant mortality, for Travellers it was found to be 2.5 times greater than the national average.[5]

More infant mortality data became available in 1995, based on an estimate of the total number of live births in Traveller families in that year. According to the Irish Sudden Infant Death Association, it showed that the occurrence of sudden infant death syndrome was 4 times higher or 2.2 versus 0.6 for the settled population per 1,000 live births.

Without doubt, this lack of basic data greatly hampers providing culturally appropriate health services for Travellers.

CULTURE

The defining characteristics of any culture are the set of ideas that a particular group of people have in common. As described sociologically, it is those habits, ideas and emotions which are most strongly held by the group. Travellers and settled people in Ireland share elements of the same culture but overall Traveller's individual culture is very separate to the settled Irish culture.

At the core of Traveller culture is family, nomadism, a distinct language, economy, shared religious values and beliefs, history and way of life.

LANGUAGE

Travellers have their own distinct language named 'cant', 'gammon' or 'shelta'. Unfortunately, there is a decline in its fluent speakers and general usage. According to a national survey of Traveller attitudes commissioned by the Citizen Traveller campaign in 2001, it found that 2 out of 10 Travellers surveyed said 'they used the language in

---

5. Health Research Board Report, 1987. [?Title]

some form every day', but of those, 8 out of 10 said 'when they spoke the language they used only a few words'.[6]

NOMADISM

Traveller's nomadic tradition is a defining characteristic of their culture and is in contrast to the sedentary or 'settled' population. How Travellers exercise that tradition has changed over time for a number of reasons, including a change in trading and economic practices and educational factors, but also for reasons related to official policy and in particular since the introduction of the criminal trespass law – Section 10 of the Criminal Justice (Public Order) Act 1994 amended by the insertion of Section 24 of the Housing (Miscellaneous Provision) Act 2002.

Despite this, some customs associated with nomadism remain and of particular relevance at times of death and illness is the response of the extended Traveller family, which is sometimes demonstrated by families travelling, gathering and pulling in together to be close to a sick or dying relative and maintaining vigils around where the person is located. However, the basic elements of the nomadic tradition are found in many aspects of Traveller culture with travelling being just one part of it.

Central to nomadism are the customs and traditions practised in relation to family life and living in groups with extended family. The concept of nomadism is sometimes the subject of negative publicity and comment by the settled population, and issues especially related to Traveller accommodation are frequently confused.

ACCOMMODATION

Planning Traveller accommodation in a consultative and culturally appropriate way is vital in meeting Travellers' needs. Where Travellers live depends on a number of factors. For many it is where the accommodation provided is culturally appropriate, that is, to live in close proximity with family and extended family. This type of Traveller-specific accommodation is commonly defined as:

- Permanent halting sites
- Group housing schemes
- Transient halting sites.

Some Travellers however live in standard local authority housing and others in private accommodation. Disappointingly, the slow progress of the implementation of the

---

6. Citizen Traveller: National Survey of Attitudes of Travellers 2001, Behaviour & Attitudes Market Research.

Department of the Environment's National Traveller Accommodation Programme has forced many Traveller families to live on roadsides throughout Ireland without access to toilets, water or electricity. At time of publishing, the latest figures available from the Annual Count of Traveller Families in Local Authority and Local Authority Assisted Accommodation and on unauthorised sites of the Department of the Environment, November 2006, showed the following:

TABLE 1.1: TRAVELLER ACCOMMODATION

Type of Accommodation	Number of Families
Standard local authority	2941
Group housing	642
Halting site	1131
Private (houses) local authority	433
Provided by voluntary bodies with LA Assistance	104
Roadside	629
Total number of Traveller families	5880

Source: Department of the Environment, November 2006. Annual Count of Traveller Families in Local Authority and Local Authority Assisted Accommodation and on unauthorised sites of the Department of the Environment.

It is widely acknowledged that there is a critical link between quality of accommodation and the health status of Travellers and that Travellers fare better across many life and health factors when their accommodation is culturally appropriate, planned in consultation with them and of good quality. In the Citizen Traveller: Traveller Attitudinal Survey of 2001[7], it substantiated this point and found that there was 'a marked disparity in Traveller's satisfaction with life depending on the type of accommodation lived in'. The highest level of *satisfaction* was found to be amongst those living in Traveller group housing schemes, whereas for Travellers living on temporary sites or on the roadside *dissatisfaction* levels rose to 40 per cent.

Other findings showed that fear of forced movement remained a concern for 44 per cent of Travellers surveyed; given the introduction of criminal trespass legislation this remains a potent worry for those 629 Traveller families living on the roadsides at this time.

---

7. Citizen Traveller: National Survey of Attitudes of Travellers 2001, Behaviour & Attitudes Market Research.

DISCRIMINATION

It is widely acknowledged that Travellers are one of the most marginalised groups in Irish society and their experience of discrimination is an everyday reality. They continue to fare poorly across a number of measuring indicators, including:

- Unemployment
- Poverty
- Social exclusion
- Health, infant mortality and life expectancy
- Education
- Access to decision and political representation
- Accommodation
- Gender equality
- Access to credit.

At institutional level, policies, procedures, services and laws have traditionally alienated Travellers by excluding either intentionally or unintentionally their needs as expressed through their separate culture. These institutional exclusions have centred on the development and formulation of polices by the majority settled population over the minority population. Policies which impinge on their culture and threaten its continuity still affect Travellers in Ireland today, and in the face of this long-standing exclusion Travellers and their representative organisations have campaigned to seek full equality in national, social and economic strata.

This nationwide Traveller movement mobilised through a partnership of both settled people and Travellers comprises over 80 organisations actively engaged in addressing marginalisation and inequality. Travellers in the process are represented at national fora and have – through this long commitment to seeking equal status – contributed to the formulation of policy and important legislative measures affecting their lives and their right to an equal place in Irish society. Some of those policies include:

1995 The Report of the Task Force on the Traveller Community

1998 Housing (Traveller Accommodation) Act

1999 Employment Equality Act

2000 Equal Status Act

2002 National Traveller Health Strategy

A very significant development in the drive for equality for Travellers was the enactment of the equal status and employment equality legislation and in turn the establishment of the Equality Authority. Through this legislation, Travellers were specifically named as a minority community and identified for protection from discrimination from institutions, policies and services in the State. Importantly, both of these Acts recognise and acknowledge Travellers' shared history and right to be nomadic.

TRAVELLER ECONOMY

Travellers have traditionally been associated with a specific economy that is based on a structure of organising labour and income-generating opportunities. Some of the features of that economy are associated with trades and services, like construction, landscaping, recycling, scrap dealing, markets and fares. Skills linked with these trades are learnt over generations and are passed predominantly from father to son, though today some of these occupations/skills have become outmoded and some Traveller families have become deskilled and are dependent on social welfare for survival.

Travellers have also been active in the mainstream labour market and economy in a range of industries and enterprises and, in particular in recent times, Traveller women especially have been working in the community, health and social development sector. According to statistics recorded among Travellers in the 2002 Census, the most popular areas of work for the Traveller labour force were in the following sectors:

- Wholesale and retail trade
- Health, social work and education
- Business activities
- Manufacturing
- Construction
- Hotel and restaurant
- Agriculture, forestry and fishing
- Community, social and personal services.

Census figures also reflect the disparities between the settled and Traveller population in terms of employment during a time of high economic growth. Figures show that of all people who identified themselves as Travellers within the Census, 73 per cent of men were unemployed compared to just 9.4 per cent of settled men.

Chapter 3

Footsteps in the Snow

Michael and Mary Hutchinson are parents to seven children and 19 grandchildren. For Mary Hutchinson a spell of ill health 18 years ago necessitated a move to Dublin to access medical care, and so she and her family relocated from their home in Cloughjordan, County Tipperary. Initially living in temporary accommodation, they were eventually moved into a house on a permanent halting site in Tallaght and have continued to live there ever since.

In November 2003, their 29-year-old son Joe committed suicide. Tragically, this followed the death four weeks earlier of his 5½ year old daughter. Joe ended his life at the back of the family's home. His father Michael found his body and described events of that time:

> I came home from work around 6am and I went down checking a few horses. The night was so dark I had a torch. I saw a sort of a white sheet or a shirt and I kept the torch on it for a moment, as I got closer to it I knew it was a body and I kept shouting 'hello, hello' and I went over and shook the body.

Mary continued:

> The last time I seen Joe he took his jacket off; I'll never forget it, he said 'Mammy, I'll leave that there and I'll be back in a minute', but he went through the door and I never seen him until his father found him the next morning.

Tragically just seven weeks after Joe's death one of Michael's and Mary's grandchildren died, and on Christmas Eve Michael made a lonely and sorrowful journey to Donegal to bring his baby grandchild's body to North Tipperary for burial, laying to rest a third offspring in less than three months.

Joe Hutchinson was a committed hurling player and a member of the local GAA team. His family describes him as a well-liked character, a storyteller with an outgoing personality and a good sense of humour, and many people gathered to pay their respects at his funeral. He was buried with his daughter in a Dublin cemetery, a deviation from the family's traditional burial place, as Michael explained:

He was buried beside his daughter in Fingal but all belonging to me is buried in Cloughjordan. I thought this over, if it happened to you you'd love to be where your child is wouldn't you. So we put him beside his child; when I go, I'll be going out there as well, beside Joe. There can be a lot of objections; sometimes it can be because when a person is from the country; well no matter where they die they're expected to go back to where they came from.

Other traditions around death include Travellers moving away from the place where the person died, but it is less practised today, according to Michael:

I was offered other houses by the Council but I said no because the only memories I have of my son are here and I'd be leaving all those behind me. But in the past quite a lot of Travelling families would burn everything out of a house and move on.

The devastating impact of suicide in particular is clearly palpable on meeting the Hutchinson family. To compound their recent experience, Michael recounted other earlier losses:

In 1977 my brother Paddy was 26 years of age. One morning my mother got up and missed him out of the house – she went looking but he couldn't be found – she didn't know but as she was walking down this laneway looking for him he was hanging over her on a tree. Five years later on a snowy night, my mother heard the door open and called my brother Jack but couldn't find him. She saw his footsteps in the snow and followed them; he was found hanging also. The first time he went up the tree the branch broke, the second time he went up he succeeded; that will tell you just how determined he was. He was 33 years old.

Like other families who have experienced suicide, Michael and Mary are struggling in the aftermath and worry about the impact on the rest of their family: 'I always keep checking when I'm at work, I keep ringing home,' Michael said. Mary added, 'I've spoken a lot to the boys and I've said suicide shouldn't be a way out for anybody's problems.'

Michael's sister Theresa has been a regular support to the family and feels strongly about the family's need for ongoing bereavement support, as she explains:

When Joe died, one of Michael and Mary's daughters became very withdrawn, wouldn't speak for a very long time and refused to eat or drink. She's still attending a doctor, sometimes when she gets into herself we actually can't help her but in order for her to get over it she must speak about it. We have told her it's ok to cry, to get angry and to make sure she knows that she is loved and that we are there for her. She has been to counselling but she needs to continue.

Mary Hutchinson watched her son's decline during the period after his daughter's death and felt helpless in reaching out to him. Joe and his wife had been separated for over five years and during most of that time his daughter had lived away with her mother. Joe became reunited with her shortly before she died and here Mary tells of the impact of her death on him:

> After Joe's daughter died, he wanted to keep working and working, to keep going, there was no stopping him he would always find something to do. He truly loved her; he would lie on the couch with her photograph on his chest sobbing his heart out. I often tried to talk to him but he just wouldn't listen, he'd just keep crying.

Coping with his grief was particularly difficult for Joe, according to Theresa:

> In Joe's case I think it was about not being able to cope with his grief. We did try to get him to talk about it but it seemed he wasn't able to accept it. I think Travellers find it difficult to really deal with grief, we know there is information out there, but there's not enough information for us. I think maybe there should be something especially for Travelling people. There's a desperate need for it but I think it's a thing that must change really amongst Travellers as well. They need to go out and get it and sometimes by not seeking that I think depression can set in.

Eventually, Mary was approached by nuns and the local Traveller Training Centre with offers of support and counselling, as she explains:

> I did it because there is only two people in the room, you and the person that's doing the counselling. You can speak about what's bothering you. I think it can lift that little bit of a load off you and you can feel sort of relieved – even though it will never be forgotten. But sometimes I feel desperate. I pity a lot of families of people that commit suicide. There can be a lot of stigma towards suicide. People round here didn't treat us any differently though, they were very good.

The closeness of the immediate and extended Hutchinson family is obvious and this no doubt helped in their grieving. However, they are conscious that some family members find it difficult to speak openly about their loss, as Michael tells us:

> There's a barrier there – that's not to be broke. When something happens like that it's always in your mind, it never leaves you. A lot of Travellers do not know there

are services available. But I don't think they would go to a clinic, like a doctor's surgery, because it's very difficult for them to go knocking on somebody's door.

Throughout their discussion, Michael, Mary and their family intersperse their story with references to occasions and situations when they encountered signs or close experiences of their bereaved. They tell these stories in an unbroken way with each being intrinsic to the events surrounding their loss, revealing the closeness many Travellers feel to the deceased and their strong belief in the extension of life beyond death. Mary recalled a situation shortly after Joe's death:

> I was sitting in the kitchen one night around Christmas and the back door handle was held down and the door was opening. That handle was held down for about 5 minutes.

Michael remembered another:

> Some time back one of my sons was in his bedroom and Joe reappeared to him with his daughter. The question he asked him was why, why did he do it. After a few minutes he just vanished. I do believe in all my heart the dead come back. It's always in Traveller's thoughts that they do come back.

The Hutchinson family home retains many memories; spread around their living room are photographs and reminders of their much-loved son and granddaughter, smiling faces on a proud sporting occasion and a Holy Communion day. In contrast to the reminders of the deceased, their home is a hive of activity and life where Michael and Mary are surrounded by children and grandchildren. Michael said:

> My daughters and the grandkids keep everyone alive. But a question that always hangs over you is, why? I pray to Joe to stop this suicide because it's so painful and hurtful to families.

Chapter 4

Ministering within an Ethnic Minority: Perceptions of a Settled Minister

FR STEPHEN MONAGHAN CM, PARISH PRIEST, PARISH OF THE TRAVELLING PEOPLE

This chapter focuses on my observations and reflections specific to death and bereavement while working with the Traveller community over the last eight years. In compiling them, I have simply tied together some of the more common threads witnessed, which I believe may support a better understanding of important aspects of death in Traveller culture. I hope these experiences will assist other priests and service providers to respond to Travellers' needs in a manner that is mindful of their cultural uniqueness.

DEATH IN A SMALL COMMUNITY

'It was as if I could hear an echo in the church, the same words that I had spoken three times before, rebounding off the walls and sounding very hollow and empty.'

In section 2, we present findings specific to death, compiled at the Parish of the Travelling People over a 10-year period, among some Travellers living in the Dublin area. The results illuminate issues affecting Travellers related to health and mortality and highlight a multi-layered and complex picture of those effects in a tight-knit community. Stark findings emerged from this data particular to young Traveller men, emphasising the urgent need for measures to address a high incidence of road traffic accidents and suicide especially. Moreover, across all causes of death, men accounted for significantly higher rates compared with women.

Examining the statistics, I can recall many of those deaths and the terrible impact they had on the Traveller community. Through our ministry we tried to extend comfort and hope to Travellers on those bleak occasions, and it is our experience that many have a deep faith that makes the prayers and Mass provide some real consolation. However, they are also a reminder of the lack of other support structures and services available to people in such tragic situations.

One of the hidden factors in the findings is the close relationships that often exist between many of those who have died and the enormous impact their deaths have on others. I can think of one woman in particular whose two sons and two grandchildren died within a couple of years of each other. Standing in front of her and the many people who had gathered in the church again on the fourth tragic occasion was one of those moments where I, like many people, began to question everything, feeling I was running on empty and not sure if I could bring the necessary consolation to the people in front of me. It was as if I could hear an echo in the church, the same words that I had spoken three times before, rebounding off the walls and sounding very hollow and empty. Feeling as numb as everyone else and unable to say anything of any great significance to the family and their many friends, I depended on the rituals and their formulas to speak to the congregation of hope and allow those words to carry us through the occasion.

It would be true to say that there is hardly a Traveller family I know who has not been affected in some way by an accidental, early or tragic death. Some, like the family mentioned above, have suffered more than others. Given that the Traveller community is quite small, news of tragedy spreads quickly and cannot fail to have a psychological impact on many people. In searching for an explanation as to why so many young people have died, some have asked if maybe there is a curse on the community that they would experience so much sadness and loss.

I have been on halting sites when bad news was delivered and I remember an occasion when news came through that some young men had been involved in a serious car crash. No one knew if they were dead or alive. Everyone around me assumed the worst – that their son, their brother, their husband was one of the injured – an expectation that someone belonging to them had been involved. I specifically remember the hysteria of one woman whose husband, brother and brother-in-law had all suffered either death or serious injury in motor accidents in the previous few years. The shock of those tragedies seemed to come right back to her and it was obvious she lived with a constant and mortal fear of losing other members of her family in the same way. I doubt she ever really had an opportunity to process those losses. Soon afterwards at the hospital, many people gathered, fearful of the news that someone close to them had been involved.

EXPRESSING GRIEF

> *'I know that the person who expresses their pain, who shouts it out for everyone in the congregation to hear spares me the task of having to put words on it, words which are often inadequate.'*

From my experience the front seats at the funeral Mass are often filled with people who are in a sort of daze; aware of why they are there and what is happening but in a space and time of their own. It is not unusual to hear members of the deceased's immediate family say they have little or no recollection of what was said on the day of the funeral.

Some studies on the human response to shock at times of death suggest that we are only allowing ourselves bit by bit to acknowledge and accept that our loved one is dead. I have witnessed mourners at funerals who seem to get that sudden glimpse of that awful reality. Occasionally, this is accompanied by a terrified scream, the calling out of the name of the deceased or a question shouted out, 'Why?' Each situation is different and people's reactions on these occasions are unpredictable; there is no proper or predictable way for the bereaved to behave. Who can say how the widow with 10 children will react or how the father whose son committed suicide will want to express his grief. My approach is to go with the flow, to allow people the space and freedom to express their grief in whatever way it emerges. Whether that's the mother who screams at me from the pews questioning why God has allowed this to happen, or the father who pulls up a chair to the coffin of his son and sits with his arms wrapped around it, sobbing and weeping throughout the entire Mass, or the group who sit placidly in the front seats in a daze at the loss of a parent.

I have listened often as people draw comparisons between settled and Traveller funerals and it seems they make judgements about Travellers when they express their grief in a raw, strongly emotional and vocal manner, I have heard people say things like: 'typical', 'undignified' or 'what would you expect'. Conversely, words like 'respectful' are used to describe a funeral where people sit quietly and attentively. They seem to believe that there is a 'dignified' way to mourn; something to do with sitting in silence, paying attention, weeping in moderation and not too loud. But I wonder, is the scream of a person crying out from grief as a physical ache in their heart and gut any less dignified than the person who sits stoically in the church? I know that the person who expresses their pain, who shouts it out for everyone in the congregation to hear, spares me the task of having to put words on it, words which are often inadequate.

There have been as many expressions of grief from bereaved Traveller families as there have been funerals and the ease with which people can express their grief in the church or graveside to me is healthy and positive. I recently read an opinion that the constant use of Jacqueline Kennedy Onassis's image and related commentary on her dignified and poised response as she mourned her husband became a model for how people in the western world should mourn in public. However, I believe it is vital that people are facilitated to grieve in a way that helps them come to terms with their loss rather than to fit some mould at what is a truly mould-breaking time.

BEING WITH THE BEREAVED

'... he responded by giving me a hug and it was one of those memorable events that make sense of some of the symbolic gestures we take for grated in our rituals.'

Visiting a family on the occasion of a tragic death is always very difficult. In general, I have known the deceased and must try to process some of my own shock and sadness before meeting the immediate family. However, now and again it is only when I arrive at the hospital that I become aware of who has died, and this is always a very shocking moment.

When going to see people on the occasion of bereavement, and more especially in the case of a sudden or particularly tragic death, I am prepared for any sort of reaction. When visiting the woman mentioned earlier and in this case on the night of her second son's death, which occurred shortly after her first son's, I had to steel myself for the visit, considering her understandable grief and anger and the possibility that she may need to vent it. I was prepared to soak up some of that, however, this was not the case and she and the family were thankful for the visit and the time spent chatting and listening with them, processing some of the awful sadness.

On another occasion, I visited a woman whose husband had committed suicide but when she saw me arriving she ran at me with a rage I had not expected. In a similar circumstance, I called to see an old man whose son had committed suicide earlier that day. He was distraught and told me in no uncertain terms to leave his house; I was a little shaken by the force of his reaction and the language he used and it was not easy being the person on the receiving end. A couple of days later at the funeral Mass, I was concerned about how he would be and made it my business to offer him the sign of peace, to which he responded by giving me a hug, and it was one of those memorable events that make sense of some of the symbolic gestures we take for granted in our rituals. It also helped reinforce the notion that the man just needed to be angry with someone and I just happened to present myself at the right time. Unfortunately, not too long afterwards he too was killed in tragic circumstances. In general, people truly appreciate a visit on the occasion of a death and will usually invite us to say prayers for their loved one. I have found it important to just sit with people at such a time, either in the silence that often descends after death or just listening to what they are saying about the deceased and responding as best I can to the questions that need to be asked, but to which so often there is no answer.

THE FUNERAL – SHOWING GOOD RESPECT FOR THE DEAD

> *'Having been with some families during these times I am aware of the pressure to make sure that certain things happen in order to show 'good respect' to the dead person.'*

Funeral arranging is mostly organised by the men in the family from buying the coffin, hiring cars, organising the plot to carrying and lowering the coffin into the grave and at times filling it in. The shovelling of earth into the grave is where I have learnt a great deal about the extended nature of the family; the people who take a turn at the shovel are often the sons, brothers, sons-in-law and nephews of the deceased. I have frequently been surprised by some of the men taking their turn only learning afterwards of the relationship they had with the deceased. These occasions serve to emphasise the complex relationships that exist between families and the impact that a death has on so many people.

It is my experience that for Travellers choosing a coffin for the deceased is a symbol of love. I remember being with a family when choosing what I thought was a very expensive coffin for their mother's burial. But I was also struck by the reason behind their decision: they loved their mother and she had done so much for them in this life that they now wanted more than anything to show their appreciation for that love by burying her in a good coffin. The cost was irrelevant; the gesture and the generosity were what was important and in this particular instance the family could afford the expense. Unfortunately, however, the desire to show such love and respect can be accompanied by some people incurring a very heavy financial debt. I know of families and individuals who have made great sacrifices in order to pay for the funeral and the headstone for their loved one. It is not something they complain about but rather something taken for granted.

The importance of a decent coffin was emphasised for me when I heard two Traveller women talking about the time they had attended a settled person's funeral. The deceased, a mother of a large family, was laid out in a very plain coffin, which shocked the two women who thought that the family must not have loved her very much to be burying her in something so cheap.

Given the emotional circumstances of death and the effects on the bereaved, organising a funeral can be very difficult. It is usual that those who were close to the deceased will want some input into the occasion, thus it can be a complicated affair for families, involving a great deal of effort to do things right for the deceased. Having been with some families during these times I am aware of the pressure to make sure that certain things happen in order to show 'good respect' to the dead person: whether that is playing a particular song, ensuring that there is a wreath of flowers from every member of the family, deciding who will carry the coffin or ensuring that all the people who need to see the remains of the deceased are facilitated to do so. If certain things do not happen, it can leave people feeling that they have failed the deceased, causing an anxiety that people can carry for a long time.

Travellers often have specific requests around funerals and burials and I believe it is not always necessary to understand exactly why, trusting instead that there is a good reason for the request and that it is significant to the people involved. We do our best to facilitate such requests, maybe looking for an insight into its significance after the event. An example is the opening of a coffin before the funeral Mass, which can be a cause of concern for people such as undertakers, sacristans and clergy. It is my experience however that quite a number of the extended Traveller family may have travelled from England or around the country and may not have made it on time to view the body at the mortuary, which is considered very important in the process of saying a final farewell. Therefore, I always try to facilitate this as much as possible, usually arranging for viewing half an hour before the funeral Mass and in certain circumstances immediately after the Mass.

I recall one occasion when an undertaker refused to open a coffin for the family, so they invited him outside to talk about financial matters. In the meantime, the lid was lifted, the body viewed and the lid replaced before the undertaker returned. He was none the wiser, but it would not have been all that difficult to facilitate the family in meeting this request.

In preparation for each funeral I celebrate, I encourage the immediate family to share some memories with me about the person who has died, where I am frequently guided in the direction of the women in the family. Now and again people will just leave it to me, telling me 'you have the words, you know what to say'. Among the most vital parts of my own preparation is ensuring I have the names of all the family and that I have the 'proper' name of the deceased. For example, if his name was Patrick, using the abbreviation of 'Pat' or 'Paddy' will not be good enough, and I do not take offence when someone comes forward during the Mass to let me know I have it wrong. The name of the person who died becomes something of a refrain throughout the removal and the Mass, repeating it at every appropriate opportunity is important and seems to offer a strong sense of comfort to people and reminds them that their loved one is now close to God. It is essential also to mention the names of all the immediate family, even if, as occasionally has been the case, there are 15 children or siblings, and also to include those of any deceased siblings or parents. Listing those deceased is often a shocking insight into the extent of death within some families. This mentioning of names not only draws people into the celebration of the Mass but names also have a very strong and significant place in Traveller culture. Hearing the name announced at the Mass is vitally important and similarly knowing that others have heard it.

Offering prayers at the funeral home or 'dead house', as it's often referred to, before the coffin is closed is important for people and a decade of the rosary is seen as the appropriate prayer at such a time. The beginning of prayers will usually calm and quieten what can be a highly emotionally charged time and facilitates the movement from the mortuary to the chapel. Standing beside many coffins, I have marvelled at the assortment of objects that have been placed in with the deceased: cigarettes, bottles of Guinness or whiskey, pictures of the family, mobile phones, indeed I remember a very disconcerting moment when a mobile phone began to ring from inside the coffin just as we were burying the person. Money is sometimes placed in the coffin symbolising that it has become valueless with the death of their loved one.

In the case of infant deaths, toys, baby bottles and items of clothing are often placed in the coffin, parents burying their child and the many plans and dreams they had for him/her. Unfortunately, such deaths are more common in the Traveller community with infant mortality rates 2.5 per cent higher than the national Irish average and findings outlined in section 2 indicate an even higher rate.

BURIAL CUSTOMS

> *'... and so at the burial the deceased's father emptied a bag of clay, carried from the family cemetery into the new grave.'*

My abiding image of celebrating Traveller funerals is the very high proportion of young bereaved widows and their children we have had to console. This is also sadly highlighted through statistics contained in chapter 5, showing a high incidence of death among young, mostly married Traveller men. Marriage statistics also support these findings and reveal that the average age for marriage among Travellers is 20 years, with most couples starting families very soon after.

When celebrating such funerals, getting the balance right and acknowledging the sadness and loss of each of the significant mourners, for example, the young widow, children, parents and siblings, can be difficult. It's at this point that the extended nature of the family becomes very obvious. At times the extended family can be collectively involved in the choice of burial site and related matters, and occasionally making burial arrangements in these situations can lead to slight tensions where strong traditions exist, dictating where a person should be buried, that is, in 'their own' cemetery, the one associated with the family name.

Sometimes the family's 'own' cemetery may be very far from where the family now reside making regular visiting of the grave difficult. In more recent times some Dublin-based families associate the city as their new home and quite a few have opted to have their people buried close to them. Nonetheless, this is a big wrench from tradition and creates a degree of anxiety and upset for older family members. I recall a widow deciding to bury her husband in Dublin to be close to his grave. The decision went against the wishes of his family and so at the burial the deceased's father emptied a bag of clay, carried from the family cemetery into the new grave. This gesture helped me recognise how deep some traditions are and how painful it is when people are faced with change.

We have occasionally experienced resentment from clergy and cemeteries in certain areas when Travellers continue to use traditional burial places, normally outside of Dublin to bury their family members. They fail to understand the importance to Travellers of burying their deceased among their own people and their strong sense of association with particular counties and towns. Indeed, I am aware of one cemetery that has significantly increased the cost of graves to try and prevent or at least discourage Travellers choosing it for their burials.

PROCESSING GRIEF AND RESPECTING CUSTOMS OF BEREAVEMENT

'For others it is something that needs to be done for the dead person which if it were not to happen, there would be a great sense of letting the dead person down...'

Sometimes I feel there is a pall of depression hanging over many Travellers I meet, where they are unable to process their grief before another tragedy descends upon them and where life is continuously forcing them to get on with things.

We believe there is a critical need for culturally appropriate counselling services to respond to Travellers' needs. We respond as best we can through pastoral contact, which in the case of bereavement is rarely confined to the funeral itself. We endeavour to meet the bereaved family in the subsequent weeks and are usually present at the different blessings, for example on the ninth day (which is customary for some families), the month's mind and the first year anniversary.

There is some uncertainty as to the origins of the ninth day blessing but the beliefs associated with it are that it is the day the soul enters heaven or the day the person is judged. For others it is something that needs to be done for the dead person, which if it were not to happen, there would be a great sense of letting the dead person down and a fear of possible consequences for the soul of the deceased. Thus the blessing offers people a degree of reassurance about the person who has died. Whatever its root, it allows people to come together again a short time after the death: to gather at the grave, to grieve, to remember the dead person and to offer prayers and hopefully gain some comfort, strength and consolation.

We perceive such contact and support as very important, and occasionally members of the parish team will travel long distances for such blessings, making the journey with people, so we are facilitating the process of grieving in a context that has significance to the family. We have also developed strong relationships with many families and our travelling with them is an expression of their inclusion of us in their family network and our solidarity with them in their grief. In order to make these blessings relevant for those attending, we have devised our own rituals and formulas.

Often when Travellers make the journey from Dublin to other counties for such blessings, they are unlikely to know the local priest and frequently feel awkward about putting a request for a blessing over the phone. Thus, they often seek out and arrive at the presbytery or local friary requesting a priest's attendance and do so with a deep-seated belief that priests will respond positively to such a request. In general, most priests willingly oblige. However, having tried occasionally, by phone, to invite a local priest to participate in such a blessing I have been saddened at the reaction of some, ranging from a total unwillingness to a begrudging agreement, leaving me fearful of the sort of reception the family will receive on the day. Having become quite protective of the community I work with, I would rather travel a hundred miles for a five-minute blessing than expose people to a hard-nosed prejudice of some members of the clergy. Similarly, I am being protective of the clergy, not wanting to allow such individuals to tarnish the high regard many Travellers hold for them.

REMEMBERING THE DEAD

'It emphasised for me the importance people put on remembering the dead and in this case how the family had created a way of including them in an important life event.'

There are a number of occasions throughout the year when people may visit the grave of a recently deceased family member, for example, on their birthday, wedding anniversary, Christmas day and on the first year anniversary. Honouring the dead in this way is crucial in the psyche of people. The first year anniversary is particularly significant and generally it is when the headstone is erected and blessed, invariably attracting a large gathering of people for the occasion. For all families it is essential that a priest is present for the blessing. Many now place a picture of the dead person on the headstone and it has become customary for those who attend to kiss the image. Recently, some families also gather around the grave for a photograph to be taken, which is then sent to absent family members or placed in a prominent location in the home. The size of headstones varies greatly according to the circumstances of the family; nonetheless, the majority of families invest a great deal of money in the headstone.

Pattern Sunday, or the annual blessing of graves around Ireland, is a highly significant day for many people, both settled and Travellers, where thousands attend the outdoor masses held in the various cemeteries each year. There seems little doubt about the importance Irish people in general attach to the memory of the dead. Travellers will journey from far and wide for this particular memorial service, even those in the United Kingdom will make it their business to get back to Ireland for the occasion. Some people who may have missed the service due to a difficulty with a ferry crossing or a flight have spoken about a real sense of disappointment at not being there; they feel as though they have let the deceased down, while those who attend often speak about feeling a sense of contentment or peace for themselves and their deceased.

Christmas day is another important occasion for remembering the dead and for visiting the graves of loved ones. On one occasion I was asked to bless the grave of some young men who had died earlier that year. I was a little surprised to meet so many people who had taken time out on such a day to come and pay their respects. People seemed to be in no hurry to leave and someone had even brought a tape recorder to play some of the favourite songs of the two men. When I asked a couple of people why they were there, they said 'since the two boys can't be with us on this day, it was important that we be with them'.

On another occasion I was invited to the house of a bride on the morning of her wedding and was immediately struck by the many photos of departed loved ones that had been placed all around the living room; people who were special and important in her life were included in the day, grandparents, aunts and uncles and others deceased. It emphasised for me the significance people put on remembering the dead and in this case how the family had created a way of including them in an important life event. Likewise, I remember sitting with a man as he watched a video containing the images of many of his family who had passed on. Their favourite songs were played over the images and he was unashamed about his sadness. Looking at those images, I was shocked at how young many of the people were, emphasising the scale of tragedy and loss many people encounter in their lives.

INFANT MORTALITY

'This is always a deeply moving moment, a last loving gesture towards the child and the most natural and obvious thing for parents to do.'

The death of a child is the most devastating and heartbreaking of all funerals to be involved in. When children die as a result of sudden infant death syndrome, I often hear older women recount the losses they suffered in similar circumstances. Devastating as the loss was, they say there was little or no time to sit down and mourn, with usually a large family to be cared for. Few of those women attended the funeral, and it is not difficult to pick up on the sense of guilt, regret and anxiety they have about what happened.

Nowadays there is a better understanding of the need to allow parents to grieve and they are encouraged to spend time being with and holding the child and to openly express their loss. Nonetheless, this modern response often conflicts with an older Traveller wisdom that encourages the parents, and in particular the mothers, not to hold the child, to dry her tears and not begrudge God the gift of this little child. Although these grieving parents will receive a great deal of support from people around them, they may require additional professional bereavement support.

When involved in the funeral of an infant, we ensure parents are always given the space to be on their own with their child in the mortuary. Before the coffin is closed they are invited to tuck the child in for the last time. This is always a deeply moving moment, a last loving gesture towards the child and the most natural and obvious thing for parents to do.

Throughout the funeral service people mostly refer to the infant or the child as an angel, which seems to give some consolation to parents, knowing that they have a little angel in heaven. However, this contradicts professional opinion in the area of infant death, where the minister and others are encouraged not to use this reference. The first time I ministered at the funeral of an infant I struggled to find the right words, afraid of saying the wrong thing, especially the reference to an angel. But again and again the mourners repeated the phrase, and speaking with the mother she described her beautiful little girl as an angel, someone special in heaven that would help her in this life. As a result, I became comfortable with the image and the phrase; nonetheless, I was aware that for the nurses and mortuary staff in attendance, it was as if I had mentioned the unmentionable and this continues to be an ongoing occurrence. Despite that, my experience of infant funerals is that no parent has ever reacted against the image of an angel but instead seems to be comforted by its use.

ORGAN RETENTION

'As there is no ceremony devised for the burial of organs we must formulate our own words, however inadequate, to bring completion to the whole mourning ritual for people.'

For parents, coming to terms with a sudden infant death is a devastating experience and the issue of organ retention compounds an already terrible situation. In the past the organs of a child deceased by sudden infant death syndrome were automatically retained without parental knowledge or consent. Nowadays hospitals (though still legally empowered to retain organs) must ensure parents are informed. This is a very sensitive situation as it is traumatic for the family and difficult also for hospital staff. I never fully appreciated it until I was with parents in that position who were distraught at their loss. In this case, hospital staff struggled to say as sensitively as possible what exactly organ retention meant, while the parents and family struggled to understand. Finally, the father asked for it to be explained in plain language and asked which organ were they referring to. I will never forget the shock on that mother's face as they were told it was the baby's brain. Whatever the reasons or benefits, this is a horrifying situation for parents. As a result, this family felt unable to bring any closure to the death of the infant until the organ release six weeks later.

As there is no ceremony devised for the burial of organs we must formulate our own words, however inadequate, to bring completion to the whole mourning ritual for people. In many circumstances it is the hospital social worker who may have to shoulder responsibility for facilitating this process. For Travellers it is vital that this little ceremony, which is usually very private, would require some religious gesture, either a prayer or a blessing with holy water.

POLICING OF TRAVELLER FUNERALS

'In one scenario the funeral of a man became something of a circus, with people drawn out to their gates to observe the procession......'

All funerals represent a sensitive time for bereaved families. When occasionally a funeral requires policing, for example, for traffic control or a report of potential trouble, extra sensitivity is required from the Gardaí. In our experience there is generally a police presence at funerals taking place outside of Dublin, often occurring as a result of notification from undertakers to local Gardaí. This is rare in Dublin except where the Gardaí have been directly requested to be in the vicinity of the graveyard, often at the request of the deceased's family. I accept there have been some very serious incidents involving Travellers at funerals, some of which we have witnessed, however, I have seen huge unnecessary blanket security thrown around towns for the arrival of a Traveller funeral, with road blocks, checkpoints and the closure of every pub and shop in town. I remember hearing one Traveller joke about the respect that settled people have for Travellers when they die that they even close down their businesses for the day. In one scenario, the funeral of a man became something of a circus with people drawn out to their gates to observe the procession and more people gathered in large groups around the town square to get a glimpse of the proceedings with, what I perceived to be, a degree of disdain.

All of the mourners I spoke to at the funeral were offended by the level of security and felt it reflected a certain prejudice towards them and, embarrassed by the amount of attention generated by the Gardaí, were happy to get away from the town after the burial. I do not know what prompted such a response from the Gardaí, but I have seen it replicated in smaller ways in other parts of the country.

On those minority of occasions when the deceased's family have requested a Garda presence, it is usually connected to a family dispute and where the deceased may be related to the two families involved, and so both may turn up in the graveyard. The presence of Gardaí in these situations is often enough to prevent any dispute arising and in such instances they have been superb, keeping a very discreet but obvious presence and being courteous and respectful to mourners. The result being that the town into which the funeral arrives is not thrown into a state of fear and the mourners are allowed to bury their loved one with dignity and respect. This is as much as people are asking for on such an occasion.

IN CLOSING

As a priest I am in a position of privilege being engaged with families during difficult circumstances in their lives, especially at times of death. Although suffering, bereavement and the human response to death is common to all people, many cultures, including Travellers, create their own death rites and customs significant to them. The challenge we face as service providers – such as clergy, Gardaí, undertakers, hospital and prison staff – is how we respond to that expression of cultural difference. Sometimes when we provide a service outside of our own cultural context we look to understand what is happening, and why it is happening. However, it is not always possible to fully understand what is happening for other people, needing instead an appreciation of the difference in its own right as being important to those bereaved. As service providers facilitating that difference in the best way we can is what we should aim to achieve.

SECTION 2

STUDY OF TRAVELLER MORTALITY

Something that strikes me very forcibly is the age at which people die and how they die.

Fr John Gallagher CM
Parish of the Travelling People (2000–2006)

Chapter 5

Traveller Mortality:
January 1995 – December 2004

As outlined earlier no comprehensive Traveller-specific health and mortality analysis has been undertaken in Ireland since the 1986 ESRI Report, which found that Traveller life expectancy was equivalent to that of settled people in Ireland in the 1940s. In 1987, a Health Research Board study also found that Travellers had higher rates for all causes of death compared with the settled community and increased rates for causes such as accidents, metabolic disorders, respiratory ailments and congenital-related illness.

While more recently the most available figures to date (2002 Census) provided information specific to the composition of the population, which continued to reflect a high birth rate and low life expectancy, there is otherwise very little information available regarding Travellers' general health and mortality.

The Parish of the Travelling People, while providing pastoral care services at times of death and bereavement, noted that issues related to the cause of death, age profile and gender of the deceased demanded further examination and to this end they compiled data specific to all Traveller deaths responded to by the Parish in the Dublin area over the 10-year period, 1995–2004.

The findings confirmed significantly high rates and a younger age profile for specific causes of death among the deceased Travellers when compared to national population statistics. While it was not possible to compare all causes of death as defined by data from the Central Statistics Office, or to comparatively analyse on a national basis, where findings were compared, it highlighted gross discrepancies. Those findings are outlined in the next chapter.

RESEARCH SAMPLE

The sample researched comprises all Traveller deaths responded to by the Parish of the Travelling people over a 10-year period in the Dublin area and **not** all Traveller deaths in the Dublin area. Data was analysed according to **gender**, **age**, and **cause of death** for each of the deceased.

DATA COLLECTION

Data was compiled using records maintained by the Parish of the Travelling People as pastoral provider to the family of the deceased. To ensure accuracy, in a small minority of cases records were rechecked directly with families of the deceased and where appropriate through records maintained at the General Register Office (register of births, deaths and marriages), Joyce House, Dublin. Consultation was also sought in some instances from the Dublin City Coroner's Office on queries specific to cause of death.

Uncertainty arose in a small minority of deaths, in relation to suicide, and as a result those deaths were recorded under the heading 'Accidental', which may therefore slightly underestimate suicide findings and should be factored in.

Cases of perinatal deaths[1], that is, mortality before 40 weeks' gestation, are included in the infant sample and account for 49 per cent of the total. However, for the purpose of further infant analysis regarding cause, age and gender the data is separated from non-perinatal deaths.

GENERAL ANALYSIS

The findings are analysed separately for **adults** and **infants**.

AGE

The sample total comprises 255 people: 48 infants and 207 adults. Infants are all people aged less than two years. Adults are all people aged two years and over.

PERIOD ANALYSED

The period analysed was from January 1995 to December 2004.

CAUSE OF DEATH

Deaths for all people aged two years and over are examined under the following causes:

- Coronary
- Stroke
- Road traffic accidents

---

1. Perinatal deaths refer to all deaths which occurred before 40 weeks' gestation.

- Cancer

- Alcohol

- Drugs

- Violent

- Accidental

- Suicide

- Genetic

- All other causes.

Deaths for all people aged less than two years are examined under the following causes:

- Congenital

- Genetic

- Bowel

- Heart

- Meningitis

- Sudden infant death syndrome (SIDS)

- Perinatal death.

ADULT SAMPLE: SUMMARY OF PRINCIPAL FINDINGS (ALL PEOPLE AGED TWO YEARS AND OVER)

- Half of all people in the sample were deceased before their 39th year

- 7 out of 10 deaths occurred in males

- Almost 4 out of 10 men were deceased before their 39th year compared with 1 out of 10 females

- 7 out of 10 people died before the age of 59 years

- Cancer was the most common cause of death for females (25%)

- Road traffic accidents were the most common cause of death among males (22%)

- Of all adults deceased as a result of road traffic accidents, 9 out of 10 were men, almost 50 per cent were aged between 15 and 24 years

- Men accounted for all but 1 drug-related deaths, all of whom were deceased before their 39th year

- All but 1 death resulting from violence were for men, almost three-quarters of whom were less than 39 years old

- 6 out of 10 accidental deaths occurred in people less than 39 years old

- Men exclusively accounted for all suicide deaths, over three-quarters of whom were aged less than 39 years

- Half of all men deceased by suicide were married

- Of all deaths resulting from other causes, 7 out of 10 occurred in females

Infant Sample: Summary of Principal Findings (all people aged less than two years)

- Of all deceased (non-perinatal) infants, 38 per cent died as a result of sudden infant death syndrome

- One-quarter of all (non-perinatal) infant deaths were caused by a genetic condition

Total Findings of Adult Sample (all people aged two years and over)

All Causes

- Coronary illness (16%) and road traffic accidents (16%) were the most common causes of death among males and females combined

- Three-quarters of all deaths occurred in men

- One-quarter of all deaths occurred in people between the ages of 25 and 39 years

- Half of all people in the sample were deceased before their 39th year and three-quarters before their 59th year

- Road traffic accidents were the most common cause of death among males (22%)

- Cancer was the most common cause of death among females.

FIG. 5.1: ALL CAUSES OF DEATH BY GENDER

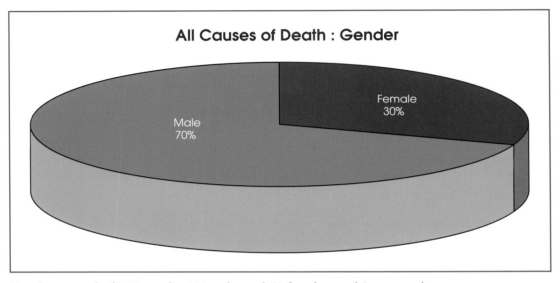

Based on a total of 207 people: 144 males and 63 females aged 2 years and over

FIG. 5.2: ALL CAUSES OF DEATH BY AGE

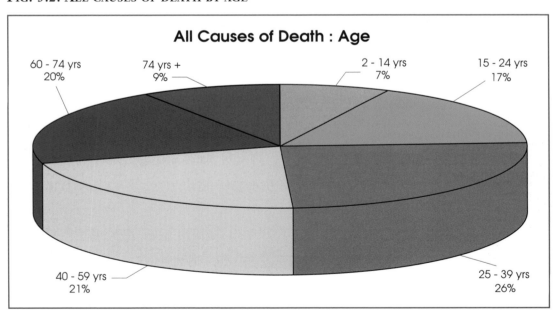

Based on a total of 207 people: 144 males and 63 females aged 2 years and over

FIG. 5.3: ALL CAUSES OF DEATH

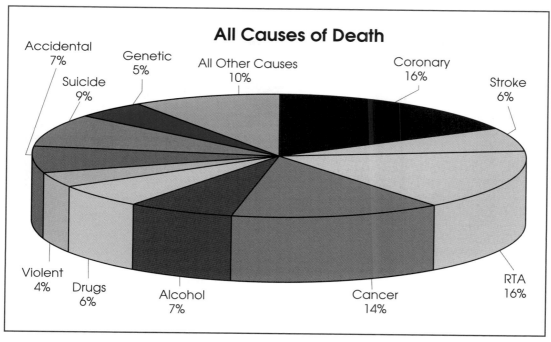

Based on a total of 207 people: 144 males and 63 females aged 2 years and over

FIG. 5.4: FEMALES BY ALL CAUSES OF DEATH

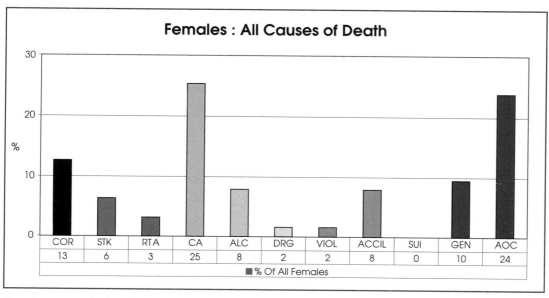

Based on a total of 63 females aged 2 years and over. See Table 5.3 for abbreviations of causes of death.

Fig. 5.5: Males by all causes of death

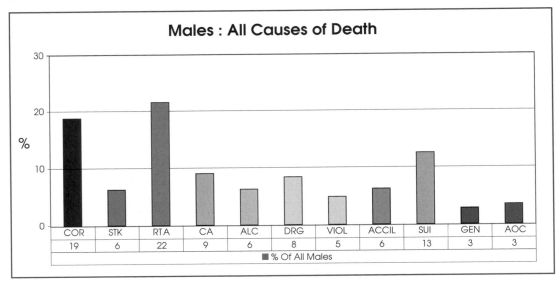

Based on a total of 144 males aged 2 years and over. See Table 5.3 for abbreviations of causes of death.

Coronary Illness

- 7 out of 10 deaths resulting from coronary illness occurred in men

Fig. 5.6: Coronary illness by gender

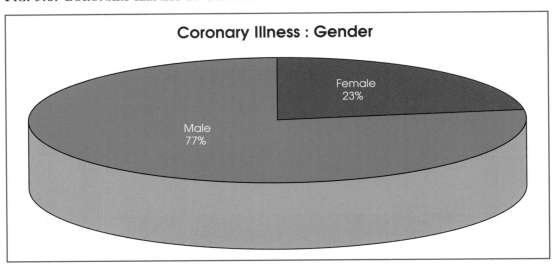

Based on a total of 35 people: 27 males and 8 females aged 2 years and over

FIG. 5.7: CORONARY ILLNESS BY AGE AND GENDER

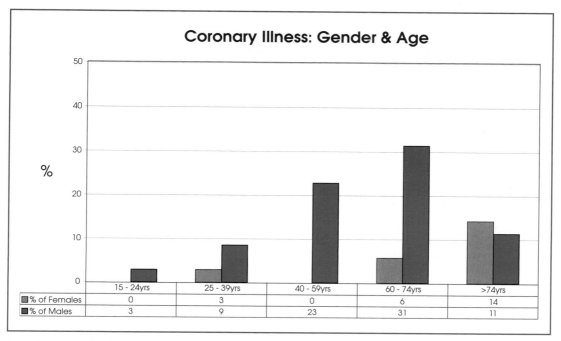

Coronary Illness: Gender & Age

	15 - 24yrs	25 - 39yrs	40 - 59yrs	60 - 74yrs	>74yrs
■ % of Females	0	3	0	6	14
■ % of Males	3	9	23	31	11

Based on a total of 35 people: 27 males and 8 females aged 2 years and over

STROKE

- Men accounted for almost three-quarters all deaths caused by stroke

FIG. 5.8: STROKE BY GENDER

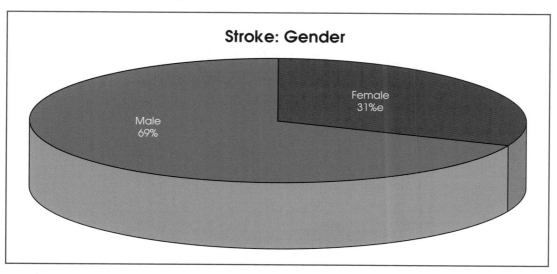

Stroke: Gender

Female
31%e

Male
69%

Based on a total of 13 people: 9 males and 4 females aged 2 years and over

FIG. 5.9: STROKE BY GENDER AND AGE

Stroke: Gender & Age

	15 - 24yrs	25 - 39yrs	40 - 59yrs	60 - 74yrs	74yrs +
% of Females	0	8	0	23	0
% of Males	0	0	15	23	31

Based on a total of 13 people: 9 males and 4 females aged 2 years and over

ROAD TRAFFIC ACCIDENTS

- All but 2 deaths resulting from road traffic accidents were male, of whom 4 out of 10 were aged between 15 and 24 years

- Over three-quarters of all road traffic accident deaths happened to motor users, that is, a driver or passenger

- Over a half of all people deceased by a road traffic accident were married

FIG. 5.10: ROAD TRAFFIC ACCIDENTS BY GENDER

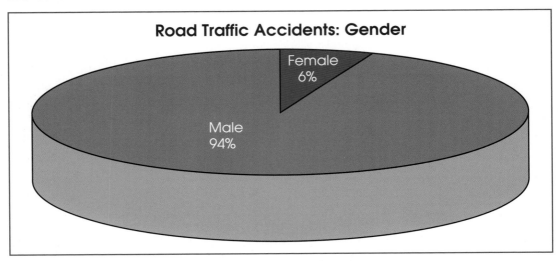

Based on a total of 33 people: 31 males and 2 females aged 2 years and over

FIG. 5.11: ROAD TRAFFIC ACCIDENTS BY GENDER AND AGE

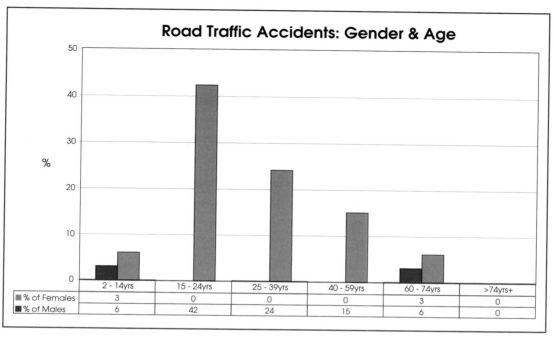

Road Traffic Accidents: Gender & Age

	2 - 14yrs	15 - 24yrs	25 - 39yrs	40 - 59yrs	60 - 74yrs	>74yrs+
■ % of Females	3	0	0	0	3	0
■ % of Males	6	42	24	15	6	0

Based on a total of 33 people: 31 males and 2 females aged 2 years and over

FIG. 5.12: ROAD TRAFFIC ACCIDENTS BY GENDER AND MODE OF ACCIDENT

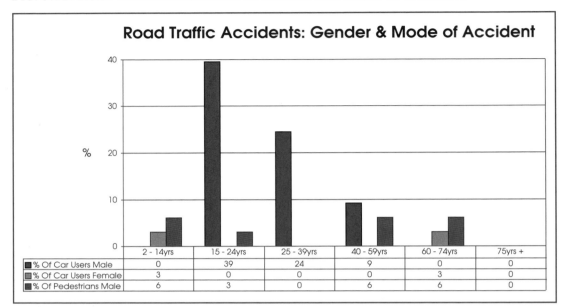

Based on a total of 33 people: 24 male car users, 7 male pedestrians and 2 female car users all aged 2 years and over

FIG. 5.13: ROAD TRAFFIC ACCIDENTS BY MARITAL STATUS

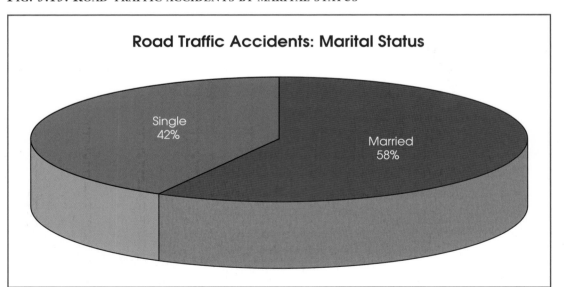

Based on a total of 33 people: 31 males and 2 females, of which 19 were married and 14 were single, all aged 2 years and over

Fig. 5.14: Road traffic accidents from 1995 to 2004

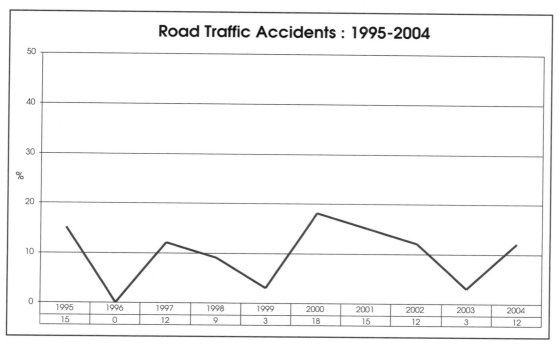

Based on a total of 33 people: 31 males and 2 females aged 2 years and over

Cancer

Fig. 5.15: Cancer by gender

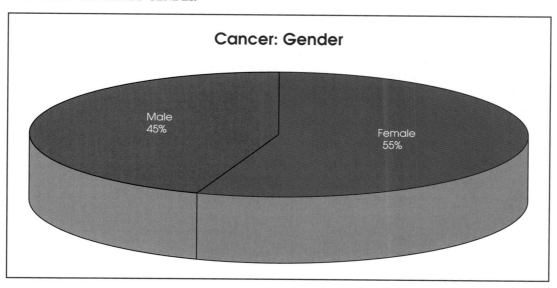

Based on a total of 29 people: 13 males and 16 females aged 2 years and over

Fig. 5.16: Cancer by gender and age

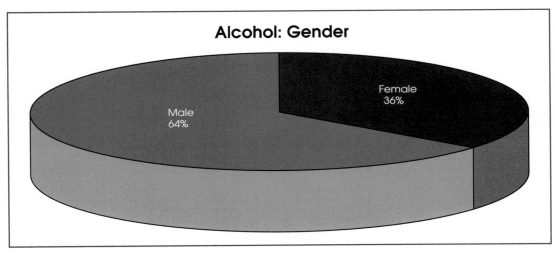

Cancer: Gender & Age

	2 - 14yrs	15 - 24yrs	25 - 39yrs	40 - 59yrs	60 - 74yrs	74yrs +
% of Females	0	0	10	34	10	0
% of Males	7	3	3	10	21	0

Based on a total of 29 people: 13 males and 16 females aged 2 years and over

ALCOHOL

- Half of all people deceased through alcohol were men younger than 40 years

Fig. 5.17: Alcohol by gender

Alcohol: Gender

Female
36%

Male
64%

Based on a total of 14 people: 9 males and 5 females aged 2 years and over

FIG. 5.18: ALCOHOL BY GENDER AND AGE

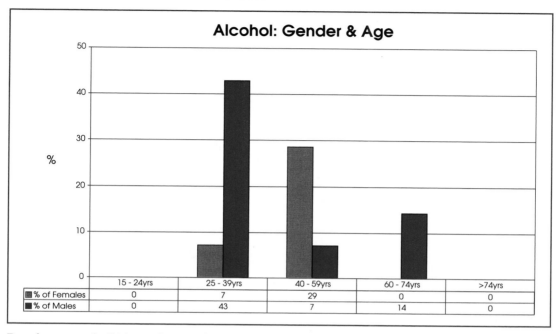

	15 - 24yrs	25 - 39yrs	40 - 59yrs	60 - 74yrs	>74yrs
■ % of Females	0	7	29	0	0
■ % of Males	0	43	7	14	0

Based on a total of 14 people: 9 males and 5 females aged 2 years and over

DRUGS

- All but one drug-related deaths were male, all of whom were aged less than 39 years

FIG. 5.19: DRUGS BY GENDER

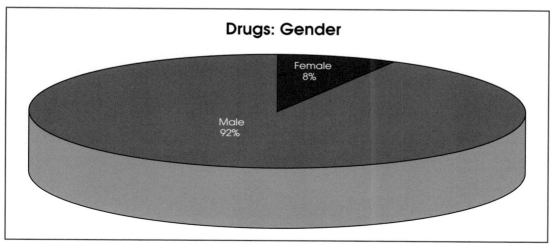

Based on a total of 13 people: 12 males and 1 female aged 2 years and over

FIG. 5.20: DRUGS BY GENDER AND AGE

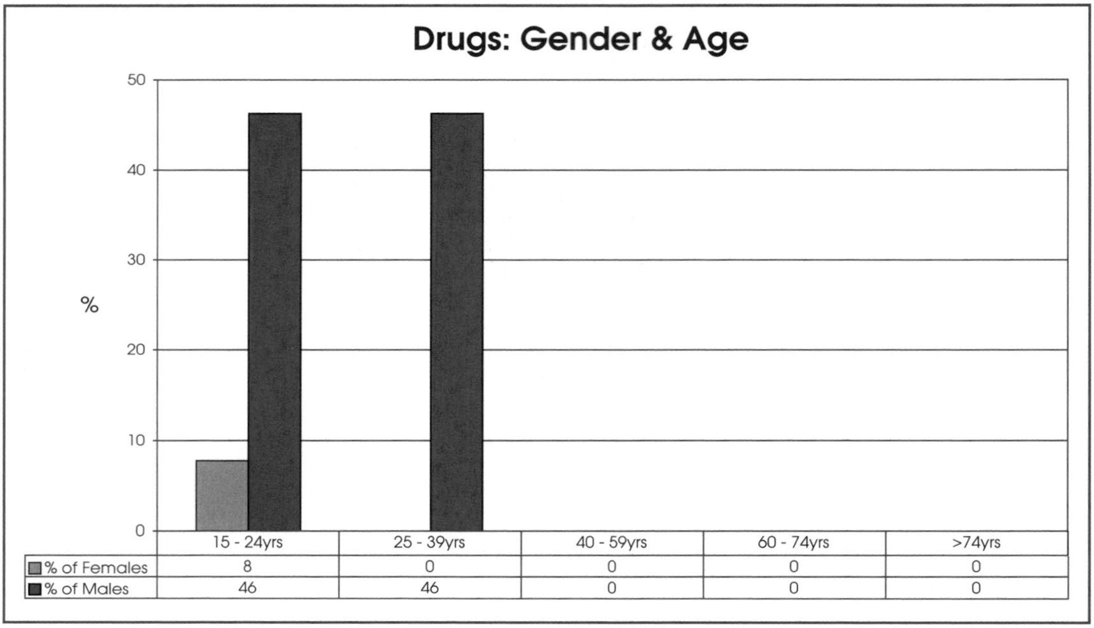

Drugs: Gender & Age

	15 - 24yrs	25 - 39yrs	40 - 59yrs	60 - 74yrs	>74yrs
% of Females	8	0	0	0	0
% of Males	46	46	0	0	0

Based on a total of 13 people: 12 males and 1 female aged two years and over

ACCIDENTAL DEATHS

- 6 out of 10 accidental deaths occurred in people less than 39 years of age

FIG. 5.21: ACCIDENTAL DEATHS BY GENDER

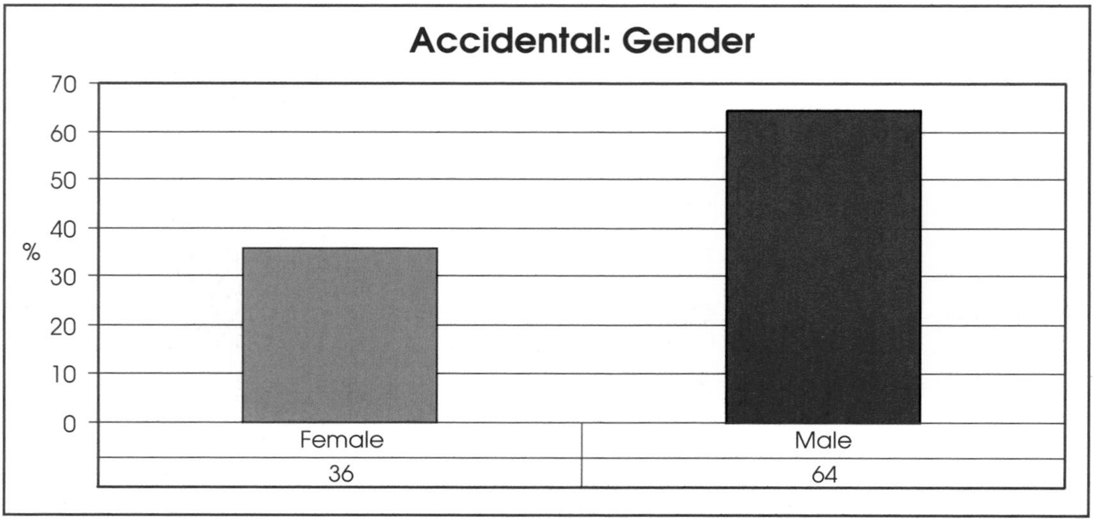

Accidental: Gender

Female	Male
36	64

Based on a total of 14 people: 9 males and 5 females aged 2 years and over

FIG. 5.22: ACCIDENTAL DEATHS BY GENDER AND AGE

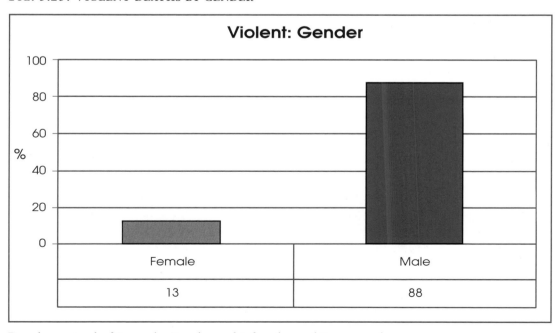

Accidental: Gender & Age

	2 - 14yrs	15 - 24yrs	25 - 39yrs	40 - 59yrs	60 - 74yrs	75yrs +
% of Females	7	0	14	14	0	0
% of Males	0	14	29	21	0	0

Based on a total of 14 people: 9 males and 5 females aged 2 years and over

VIOLENT DEATHS

- All but 1 violent deaths were male, almost three-quarters of whom were less than 39 years

FIG. 5.23: VIOLENT DEATHS BY GENDER

Violent: Gender

Female	Male
13	88

Based on a total of 8 people: 7 males and 1 female aged 2 years and over

FIG. 5.24: VIOLENT DEATHS BY GENDER AND AGE

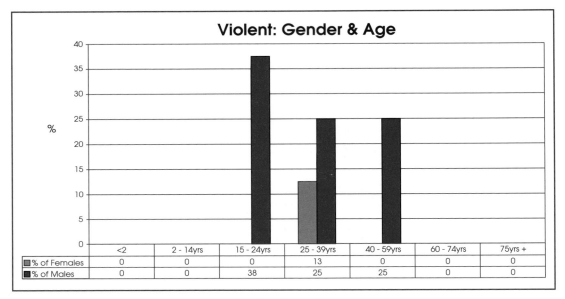

Based on a total of 8 people: 7 males and 1 female aged 2 years and over

SUICIDE

- All suicide deaths were male, over three-quarters of whom were less than 39 years and most notably were aged between 25 and 39 years

- Hanging was the most common method of suicide used, representing three-quarters of the sample

- Half of all men deceased by suicide were married

FIG. 5.25: SUICIDE BY GENDER

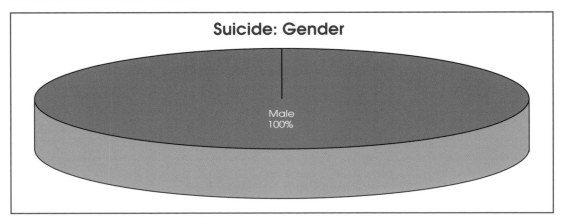

Based on a total of 18 males aged 2 years and over

FIG. 5.26: SUICIDE BY AGE

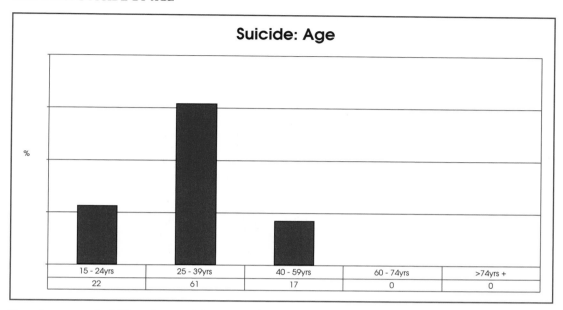

Based on a total of 18 males aged 2 years and over

FIG. 5.27: SUICIDE BY MODE

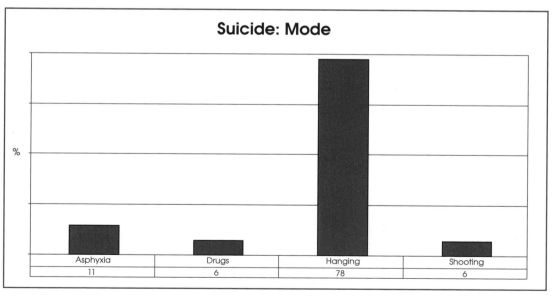

Based on a total of 18 males aged 2 years and over

FIG. 5.28: SUICIDE BY MARITAL STATUS

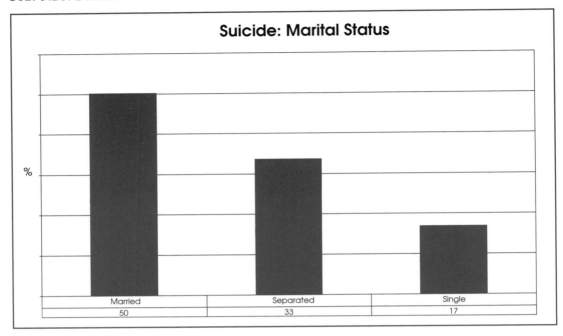

Based on a total of 18 males aged 2 years and over

FIG. 5.29: SUICIDE BY MONTH OF YEAR

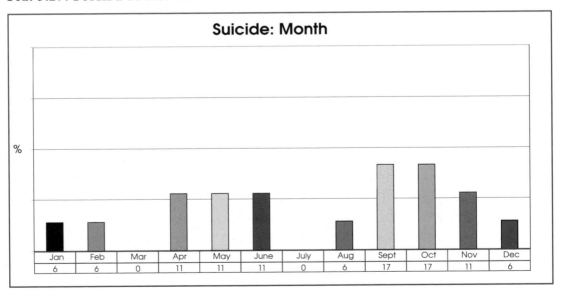

Based on a total of 18 males aged 2 years and over

Fig. 5.30: Suicide by trend (1995–2004)

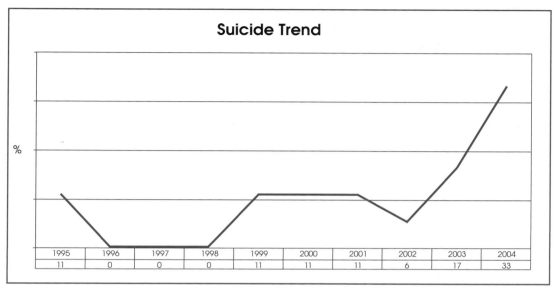

Based on a total of 18 males aged 2 years and over

Genetic Disease

- Of all people deceased through genetic disease, almost three-quarters were less than 14 years of age

Fig. 5.31: Genetic disease by gender

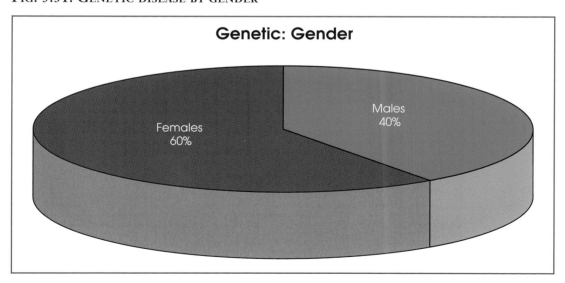

Based on a total of 10 people: 4 males and 6 females aged 2 years and over

FIG. 5.32: GENETIC DISEASE BY GENDER AND AGE

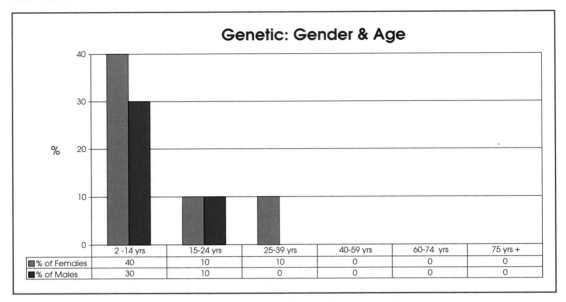

Based on a total of 10 people: 4 males and 6 females aged 2 years and over

ALL OTHER CAUSES

- Unlike other cause categories which mainly comprised a high proportion of males, three-quarters of all deaths from other causes were female

FIG. 5.33: ALL OTHER CAUSES BY GENDER

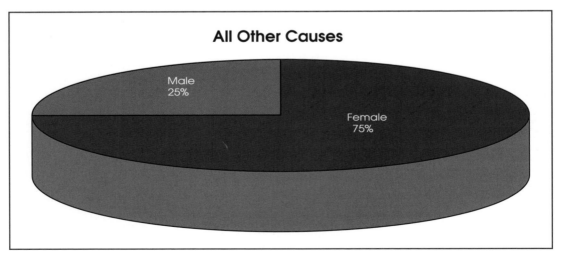

Based on a total of 20 people: 5 males and 15 females aged 2 years and over

Fig. 5.34: All other causes

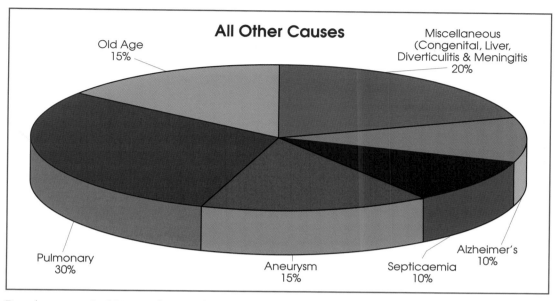

Based on a total of 20 people: 5 males and 15 females aged 2 years and over

Table 5.1: All other causes by cause, gender and age

Cause	Gender	2–14 yrs	15–24 yrs	25–39 yrs	40–59 yrs	60–74 yrs	75 yrs +
Alzheimer's	Female						2
Septicaemia	Female	1				1	
Aneurysm	Female			1	1	1	
Old age	Female						2
	Male					1	
Pulmonary	Female					3	1
	Male					2	
Misc.	Female	1					1
	Male		1			1	

These were based on actual numbers: of 20 people there were 5 males and 15 females aged 2 years and over.

TOTAL FINDINGS OF INFANT SAMPLE (ALL PEOPLE AGED LESS THAN TWO YEARS)

The following findings relate to the analysis of the total infant sample, that is, all people aged less than 2 years. Figure 5.35 includes all infants deceased pre- and post-40 weeks' gestation; however, all of the other infant findings are separated after Figure 5.35 to show causes of death, gender and age for infants born after 40 weeks' gestation.

- 38 per cent of infants, non-perinatal, died as a result of sudden infant death syndrome

- One-quarter of all non-perinatal infant deaths was caused by a genetic condition

FIG. 5.35: INFANTS BY GENDERS KNOWN AND UNKNOWN

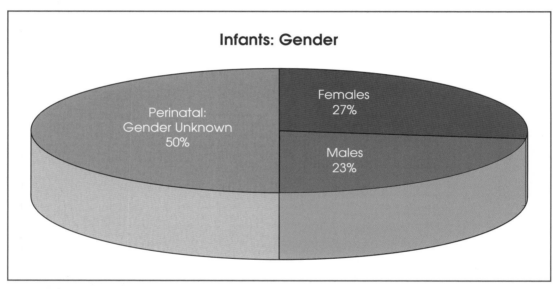

Based on a total of 48 infants: 11 males, 13 females and 24 genders unknown aged less than 2 years

FIG. 5.36: INFANTS BY GENDER KNOWN

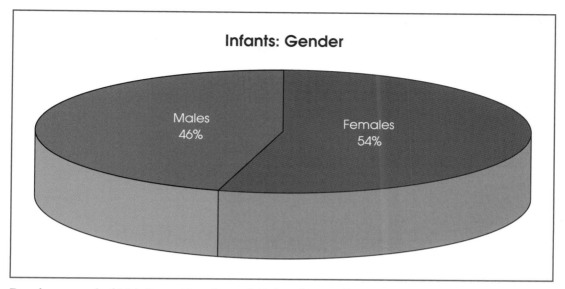

Based on a total of 24 infants: 11 males and 13 females aged less than 2 years

FIG. 5.37: INFANTS BY CAUSE OF DEATH

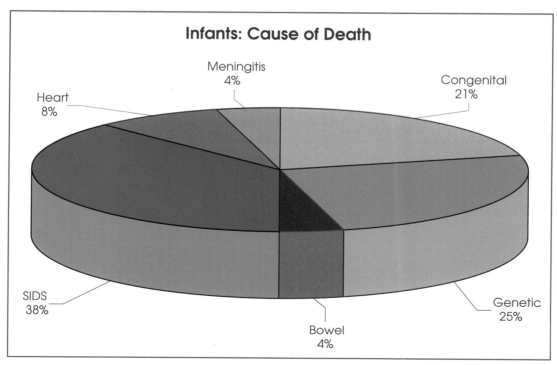

Based on a total of 24 infants: 11 males and 13 females aged less than 2 years

TABLE 5.2: INFANT MORTALITY BY CAUSE, GENDER AND AGE

Cause	Gender	<28 days	4-8 weeks	9-16 weeks	17-24 weeks	25-52 weeks	>52 weeks
Congenital	Female	2		1			1
	Male			1			
Genetic	Female						1
	Male	1		1		1	2
SIDS	Female	1	4	2	1		
	Male			1			
Meningitis	Male					1	
Heart	Male		1			1	
Bowel	Male	1					

These are based on actual numbers, of 24 infants there were 11 males and 13 females aged less than 2 years.

TABLE 5.3: ABBREVIATIONS OF CAUSE OF DEATH

Cause of death	Abbreviation
Coronary	COR
Stroke	STK
Road traffic accidents	RTA
Cancer	CA
Alcohol	ALC
Drugs	DRG
Violent	VIOL
Accidental	ACCIL
Suicide	SUI
Genetic	GEN
All other causes	AOC

Chapter 6

Traveller Data vs. National Population Statistics

In this chapter we compare some key data on Traveller deaths against the closest equivalent data based on national statistics. In making these comparisons we have drawn the national data from the Statistical Yearbook of Ireland 2006.[1]

The data on Traveller deaths reported here are based on all Traveller deaths reported to the Parish of the Travelling People in Dublin over a 10-year period. It is important to bear in mind that the information does not relate to *all* Travellers living in Ireland. It does not even relate to the total Traveller population of the greater Dublin area. It is confined purely to those deaths reported to the Parish. Over the 10-year period under review, there were 231 such deaths reported, excluding those infants deceased before 40 weeks gestation.

DIFFERENCES BY GENDER

For the population as a whole, the number of deaths reported in any given year is likely to be made up about equally of men and women.

For the past few years, the percentage split has been as follows:

TABLE 6.1: PERCENTAGE OF DEATHS PER GENDER (2001-2005)

General population: deaths by gender		
Year	Male	Female
2005	50.7%	49.3%
2004	51.5%	48.5%
2003	51.2%	49.8%
2002	51.9%	48.1%
2001	51.9%	48.1%

---

1. Produced by the Central Statistics Office (CSO).

It can be seen that there is a considerable degree of consistency from one year to the next. The average shows a slight preponderance of males (approx. 51/52%). The data for Travellers is in marked contrast to the above data. Over the 10-year period under review, the gender split was as follows:

- Travellers' deaths by gender:
  - ➤ Male   67%
  - ➤ Female   33%

There is clearly something distinctive about the pattern of Traveller deaths with a higher than expected incidence among males.

DEATHS BY AGE GROUP

There is an even greater disparity in the pattern of deaths by age group as between Travellers and the general population. The relevant comparisons are as follows:

TABLE 6.2: DEATHS ANALYSED BY AGE GROUP

Deaths analysed by age group		
	Travellers	Total Population
	%	%
Under 2	10	1.0
Over 2-14	7	0.3
15-24 years	15	1.3
25-34 years	15	1.6
35-44 years	10	2.4
45-54 years	12	5.1
55-64 years	12	10
65+ years	19	78.3
	100	**100**

It can be seen that only 2.6 per cent of all deaths occurring among the total population are accounted for by people aged under 25. In the Traveller data reported to the Dublin Parish, the equivalent percentage is 32 per cent. The implication here is that the disparity in deaths among Travellers is age as well as gender specific. There is a higher than average death rate among *younger* Travellers and among *younger* males in particular.

We can gain a better understanding of why this may be so if we examine data on the causes of death.

CAUSE OF DEATH COMPARISONS

Cause of deaths statistics are normally calculated as a rate per 100,000 population. Direct comparisons are problematic because of the difficulties referred to earlier and also because the records are not kept using exactly the same classifications. However, it is possible to make some broad comparisons and these suggest the following:

TABLE 6.3: DEATH RATES PER ANNUM PER 100,000 POPULATION

DEATH RATE PER ANNUM PER 100,000 POPULATION Travellers in Dublin vs. Total Population		
	Dublin Travellers	Total Population
Cause of death	Deaths per 100,000	Deaths per 100,000
Road traffic accidents	63.7	6.5
Suicide	34.7	10.4
Accidental	27	22.4
Coronary or stroke	92.6	*241.7
Cancer	56	184.3
*Deaths of the circulatory system		

- Death rates are particularly high (by the standards that one might expect based on general population statistics) for Travellers in the areas of road traffic accidents, suicides and, to a less marked extent, accidental deaths generally.

- Traveller deaths as a result of cancer and heart disease are at a significantly *lower* rate than the average for the population. This, of course, is a function of the fact that Travellers are dying much younger and from a particular set of causes as identified in the table.

This is not however the full explanation of the age-based differences discussed earlier. If one checks back to Table 6.2 it can be seen that 10 per cent of all Traveller deaths occur among infants (those aged under 2). The comparable figure for the general population is only 1 per cent. In part, at least, these disparities can be explained by differences in the incidence of sudden infant death syndrome[2] as discussed below:

During the 10-year period under review there were nine reported instances of sudden infant deaths among the Traveller community *who attended at the Dublin Parish*. For the total population (i.e. the general public, throughout the Republic of Ireland) there were 349 such deaths over the same period.

In the following table we relate these sudden infant deaths to the total number of estimated births for Travellers and for the general public for the country as whole.

TABLE 6.4: SUDDEN INFANT DEATHS PER TOTAL POPULATION AND PER ESTIMATED TRAVELLER BIRTHS

Sudden Infant Death Syndrome			
	Travellers	General Public	Travellers as % of Total
Number of births	6,820	570,000	1.196
Number of Sudden Infants Deaths	9	349	2.578
SID/rate per 1,000 pop.	1.320	0.612	2.15*

Multiplier

It must be stressed that the figures in this table relate to the total population throughout the country in all cases *except* for the sudden infant death figures for Travellers. These relate *only* to the deaths as presented to the Parish in Dublin and must therefore be seen as a very significant understatement. Even allowing for that, it can be seen that the estimated rate of sudden infant deaths among Travellers is more than double the national average.

Only 22 per cent of Travellers live in the greater Dublin area (according to the 2002 Census). The *national* figure for sudden infant deaths is therefore likely to be four or five times the Dublin figure. The obvious implication is that the rate of sudden infant death among Travellers may be as high as 8 to 10 times the national average.

---

2. Based on statistics from the Irish Sudden Infant Death Association.

SECTION 3

RECOMMENDATIONS

In nursing I would probably approach a Travelling person the same way I would a settled person, it wouldn't come into my thinking that I'm going to do this in any different way; which maybe is something that should be. I'm sure there are issues that we are not aware of.

Participant, Service Provider Focus Group

Chapter 7

Recommendations: Hospital Services

POLICY AND TRAINING

In compiling this book it was widely reported by service providers that they had acquired their knowledge of Travellers through contact with them in their workplace. None reported receiving in-service training or diversity-specific information from their employer. Following further consultation with some hospitals in the Dublin area in 2006, a lack of diversity policies was found in all but an exceptionally small minority. Where policies did exist, they were in the early development stage and responded to an increase in numbers of multi-ethnic patients. Furthermore, among that minority some hospitals had introduced diversity in the workplace training, mainly resulting from the growth of a multinational staff team.

Where policies were in place, almost all did not identify Travellers as a separate culture or focus on their particular cultural needs, perpetuating a policy of alienating Travellers by their distinct lack of reference.

UPTAKE OF HOSPITAL SERVICES

The UCG/McCarthy Report of 1995,[1] concluded that 35 per cent of Travellers reported that they experienced discrimination while using hospital services. It also found that Travellers have a low uptake of inpatient hospital services, indicating a number of contributing factors further outlined in chapter 8.

> 'For Traveller patients sometimes 30 or 40 people can visit on these meagre facilities and that can be problematic. We are cognisant that this is important in Traveller culture and (we) expect people to come from far distances to see their relative and we do our best to facilitate that.'
>
> *Evelyn McElligott, Nurse Manager, Neurological Intensive Care Unit (ICU), Beaumont Hospital*

Having access to and a positive experience of hospital services is especially important to Travellers. Frequently, contact with a hospital may be the last port of call for a Traveller

---

1. The research report *Health Service Provision for the Travelling Community in Ireland, 1995* was based on a sample population study of Travellers' use of hospitals and general practitioner services. Produced by the Centre for Health Promotion Studies, University College Galway/Patricia McCarthy and Associates, 1995.

patient and often in the circumstance of advanced ill health. Travellers' alienation from health services and other factors which are attributed to a lack of uptake of services can sometimes affect their knowledge of how services, facilities, systems and resources operate at hospitals, thus creating additional frustration for them on the perceived limits of the service being provided.

LITERACY

Travellers and service providers report that poor literacy is a further barrier both to the provision of and uptake of services. Poor literacy was also found to compound Travellers' fears of contact with health, hospital and doctor services. The most commonly reported literacy difficulties outlined in the UCG/McCarthy Report related to comprehension problems regarding patient diagnosis, the prescription and administration of medications and treatments, and difficulties understanding medical conditions. Some Dublin hospitals that were consulted for the purpose of this book showed that there was a common lack of literacy support aids, and in a small minority of cases where assistance was available it was presented in the form of language aids used to facilitate non-English-speaking patient groups.

> 'There are people out there who are extremely embarrassed about their literacy skills and they will hide it as much as possible. It's not just funerals, when they are going into hospitals or even their GP, they are extremely nervous about going. My advice to them always is 'two of you go and if one picks up what is being said ... 'It is very traumatic and they have a fear of doctors, hospitals and anything to do with their health. They are not hearing what the doctors are saying. They are using medical jargon that confuses them.'
>
> Participant,
> Service Provider Focus Group

As a background to general population literacy levels in Ireland, we can refer to the most recent information available, the 1995 International Adult Literacy Survey compiled in conjunction with the Organisation for Economic Co-Operation and Development (OECD). The OECD carried out the first ever multinational assessment of adult literacy assessing the profile of literacy skills of adults aged between 16 and 64 years. Based on the premise that all adults are literate to some degree, it sought to question not 'Can you read?' but 'How well can you read?' Results were measured on a scale of 1–5, with Level 1 being the lowest level, indicating very low literacy skills and where the individual may, for example, have difficulty identifying the correct amount of medicine to give to a child from the information found on the medicine package.

Findings from Ireland revealed that 1 in 4 Irish people were found to score at Level 1,[2] the lowest level.

---

2 Literacy statistics available from the National Adult Literacy Agency (NALA).

Though there are currently no statistics available specific to Travellers and literacy, it is generally accepted on the basis of educational indicators and feedback from practitioners and educators that a far higher proportion of Travellers rate at what has been defined as Level 1.

PRACTICES OF CULTURAL VALUE

Travellers and service providers consulted report a general lack of knowledge concerning the traditions practised by Travellers at occasions of illness and death and which occur in the hospital setting. While there was some familiarity by hospital staff with the Traveller family's response on the admission of a sick relative and the subsequent gathering of the extended family to maintain a vigil, this was perceived by some as an obstacle to service provision rather than an aspect of culture. A further perception was that it impacted negatively on the smooth running of services.

> 'I'm sure it is probably the same in every hospital but I know we recently appointed a cultural diversity officer for our non-nationals, whereby we made a folder on cultural diversity, and it has every culture and religion and their beliefs, their needs and what have you set out. Our Travelling community are not set down as a separate culture.'
>
> *Participant,*
> *Service Provider Focus Group*

On the issue of hospital facilities some Travellers and service providers consulted report better family and visiting facilities in hospitals in the UK compared with Ireland, where for example visitor and family facilities are common to most hospitals and are in keeping with a series of family-centred responses. Travellers specifically felt that there they received better treatment, a more culturally appropriate response and access to good facilities and culturally trained staff. On the other hand, basic facilities for families surrounding even the most critical care points in most Irish hospitals are dismal or non-existent, in some cases where visitors maintain vigils on corridors for often days at a time.

It could be said that the insufficiencies referred to relate to a general dearth of equitable and inclusive policies and concur with the broad reportage on the state of the Irish health system. Consultations with the main Dublin hospitals point to a generally pervasive picture of inadequacies with regard to diversity policies; nevertheless, a minority of individual hospitals has given some attention to the issue. A recent response by one Dublin hospital was the appointment of a cultural diversity officer and the development of information packs for staff related to culture, religious beliefs, customs and traditions. Unfortunately, while this was a progressive action identifying a broad-reaching range of cultures, it again failed to include Travellers as a target group.

RELIGIOUS AND HEALING PRACTICE

It is generally observed that many Travellers place an emphasis on religious relics, blessings, cures, holy people and healers, particularly during times of illness where it is common to surround a sick relative with these symbols. However, most service providers consulted did not understand the practice.

'There was a young lad not well not too long ago and they were coming from everywhere and they would bring back whatever cure they might have. There could be all kinds of things ... the faith healer would have to come in person to the sick person and deliver that to them. Sometimes the nurses have stopped people from going in.'

Participant, Traveller Focus Group

HOSPITAL CHAPLAINCY

Hospital chaplains often provide a vital link between Traveller patients, their families and hospital staff, especially in situations of terminal care. In ongoing discussions, Travellers found this to be an invaluable service, however, they reported inconsistencies among hospitals. Travellers also report a lack of follow-up after discharge, especially regarding support or referral to onward services.

Perhaps unsurprisingly, Travellers' perception of hospital chaplaincy is more positive where there was an understanding of culture and religious observances.

RECOMMENDATIONS: POLICY AND TRAINING

While the recommendations contained here are specific to illness and death, they are made in recognition and in support of the recommendations contained within the report, *Traveller Health – A National Strategy 2002–2005*, especially those relevant to hospital services.

1. The development and adoption of diversity policies by hospitals that positively name and target Travellers is vital in order to fundamentally improve their engagement with and uptake of services and is imperative in the provision of more equitable and culturally appropriate services in the healthcare sector.

2. The appointment of culturally trained staff is at this time more than ever crucial in order to cater to a diverse patient population, including Travellers as a distinct patient group.

3. Without comprehensive diversity policies, practical and immediate steps addressing diversity issues could include the adoption of anti-racism and intercultural training for all hospital personnel, and it is highly appropriate that Recommendation 118 contained within *Traveller Health – A National Strategy 2002–2005* should be

advanced as soon as possible, as follows: 'Hospital staff who regularly come into contact with members of the Traveller community will receive training and education in intercultural and anti-discrimination practices and in particular Travellers' perspectives on health and illness.'

RECOMMENDATIONS: LITERACY

1. Given the prevalence of poor literacy levels in Ireland, rectifying the gaps which currently exist in this regard in hospitals is essential, thus improving Traveller's equality of access and contributing to more positive outcomes for service user and provider.

> 'When there is someone sick, the amount of Travellers that will visit them regardless of anything. A lot of them would be related, they would be close related. There could be 100. They would all show up, making sure that they were thinking about you in the hospital.'
>
> *Participant, Traveller Focus Group*

2. Practical starting points could include the appointment of culturally trained representatives to liaise with patients and families responding to queries and ensuring clarity in the delivery of patient information. Other simple interventions might include the use of symbols in addition to text on all patient literature, colour-coded directional signage, and the option to designate alternative postal addresses, for example, to a public health nurse office or other community support representatives for hospital correspondence, etc.

RECOMMENDATIONS: PRACTICES OF CULTURAL VALUE

1. Travellers commonly respond to the news of a person being hospitalised, particularly where there is a threat of fatality, in the gathering of the immediate and extended family. No doubt, at some level the physical impact of a gathering of a large group of people is felt on the hospital's amenities, often straining contact between Traveller visitors and hospital staff. Where these challenges arise, they could be assisted by a hospital cultural liaison officer who could facilitate consultation, liaison and support.

2. In this regard, it is also highly appropriate that Recommendation 119 of *Traveller Health – A National Strategy 2002–2005* be implemented, as follows: 'The feasibility of appointing appropriate liaison persons in hospitals to address issues relating to Traveller use of hospital services will be examined.'

3. Similarly, in the absence of other broad-reaching strategies, the hospital-patient representative system, available in some hospitals, could be used to support Traveller patients and their families interact with hospital services and improve points of contact.

RECOMMENDATION: RELIGIOUS AND HEALING PRACTICE

1. Unfamiliarity with cultural observances as mentioned earlier is common among hospital staff, highlighting a need for in-service training. At the very least cultural information packs should be provided for all frontline staff, helping to reduce the information deficit and provide for a more positive engagement between Travellers and hospital personnel. Consultation with Traveller organisations in the provision of training could be a valuable approach to adopt. Cultural liaison staff could also be helpful on these specific matters and more appropriately recognise and respond to issues.

RECOMMENDATION: HOSPITAL CHAPLAINCY

1. It is common for hospital chaplains to develop a closeness to a patient and their family when responding to their needs around critical times of illness and death. Nonetheless, occasionally there are needs which cannot be met by chaplains or which require a longer-term approach or a specific intervention. In these instances it is vital that chaplains facilitate referrals to onward appropriate services.

CONCLUSION

It would be too simple to explain away Travellers' difficulties with accessing hospital services as being solely related to the well-documented shortcomings currently prevailing in the health sector. The reality is that Travellers have long experienced an alienation from health services for a variety of reasons, most of which are not related to a lack of funding or a shortage of hospital beds but for other issues (outlined in chapter 8), which have created challenges to their equality of access and their uptake of services. On the other hand, Travellers have sometimes been criticised for their lack of recognition of the systems, procedures and structures operating in hospital services.

Either way it can be said that until the publication of *Traveller Health – A National Strategy 2002–2005*,

'When attending to a terminally ill patient in hospital it is usual that large numbers of Travellers will gather to pray and be with their dying relative or friend. Some hospitals have been very understanding in such situations, while others immediately go into panic mode calling on security to manage a 'potential problem', while in fact there is no 'potential problem'. The gathering of such numbers is sometimes misunderstood. When a hospital has a good understanding of Traveller culture, it is very helpful to everyone.'

Fr John Gallagher CM,
Parish of the Travelling People
(2000–2006)

there was no comprehensive attempt by previous governments or health agencies to identify Travellers' specific needs, improve their access to services or provide appropriate responses. Improvements to policy and practice will only come about through real commitment by all sections and services of the healthcare sector, individual and collective, and through positively targeting Travellers as a patient group.

Chapter 8

Recommendations:
Suicide and Mental Health Services

More than 300,000 Irish people suffer from depression.

AWARE [1]

Considering there has been no comprehensive Traveller health analysis carried out in Ireland since 1987[2] to discuss issues related to mental health and suicide in the Traveller population, we refer to other sources, specifically data compiled by the Parish of the Travelling People, findings from AWARE, the national organisation for the support of depression, and on results established through a national settled population survey commissioned by the Irish Health Boards (precursor of the Health Service Executive).

According to AWARE, one in four men and one in two women will experience depression at some point in their lives; however, depression represents just one diagnostic category of mental illness. In the latest report from the Health Research Board, *Activities of Irish Psychiatric Services 2003*, it stated that three diagnostic groups accounted for two-thirds of all psychiatric admissions in Ireland: depression 33 per cent, schizophrenia 18 per cent and alcoholic disorders 15 per cent. [3]

The determinants of depression have factors common to both Travellers and settled people; however, Travellers as indicated earlier experience worse outcomes on almost all general health indicators in comparison to settled people, with other contributing factors such as poor living conditions. It would be fair then to assume that these poor life factors may also contribute to a higher incidence of depression and it could be further assumed that Travellers' alienation from mental health services and the challenges presented in accessing support worsen their situation.

---

1. The national organisation for the support of depression.
2. A proposal for which was included in *Traveller Health – A National Strategy 2002–2005* but no findings are available at time of print.
3. *Activities of Irish Psychiatric Services 2003*. Dublin: Health Research Board, 2003.

Travellers' lack of uptake of mental health services was included in the report *Traveller Health – A National Strategy 2002–2005*, and concluded that various issues contributed to this situation, stating:

> This may be due to a combination of inappropriate provision and a lack of awareness or confidence among Travellers in relation to the services. Other problems include poor compliance with medication (due to literacy difficulties), early self discharge against medical advice, poor attendance at follow up clinics, difficulty in providing services to nomadic families and difficulties in hospitals when large groups of relatives come to visit.

Taking into consideration the issues described it could be said that many Travellers living with and affected by mental illness are likely to be 'falling through the net' when it comes to proper diagnosis and referral to appropriate services.

SUICIDE

In 2001, a study of suicide in Ireland was commissioned by the chief executive officers of the Irish Health Boards 'to establish the incidence and associated risk factors of suicide nationally, and on a health board basis, so as to inform the present knowledge base on suicide and to facilitate the future planning of a suicide prevention programme'.

> '...there is a fairly high rate of tragedy and what amazes me is their ability to cope with such tragedy. You meet some families that just have one tragedy after another. I think it is just because they have so much of it in their lives; they become immune to it in some way.'
>
> *Participant,
> Service Provider Focus Group*

The subsequent report found that 'in recent years in Ireland, suicide has become the principal cause of death in men aged 15 to 34 years, surpassing the number of deaths from road traffic accidents'.[4]

Furthermore, according to the report's findings, almost five times more men than women died from suicide, and mental health disorders, especially depression, was identified as the highest risk factor. Other factors included alcohol-related problems, unemployment, marital status and relationship difficulties.

Data compiled by the Parish of the Travelling People (see section 2) compared with findings of the National Suicide Study showed similarities and concurred specifically on

4. *Suicide in Ireland – A National Study 2001*. Departments of Public Health on behalf of the Chief Executive Officers of the Health Boards, 2001.

gender and age. It found that the highest number of suicides occurred in young *men* between the ages of 15 to 34 years. The Traveller-specific data recorded no female death by suicide in the time analysed but found an ongoing rise in suicide amongst young men, a cause of growing concern within the Traveller community and in Ireland generally.

While it is not possible to identify common risk factors, as Travellers were not researched specifically for the National Suicide Study, it is possible to identify indicators specific to them through the demographics, cultural variables and social structure of the Traveller community, which is significant. One example of specific cultural factors is demonstrated in the marital status of young Traveller men who committed suicide, which found they were more likely to be married with children (50%) compared with the National Suicide Study which found higher rates of suicide in single (57%), separated (8%), divorced (1%) or widowed men (2%) versus cohabiting and married men (25%).

The resulting consequence of suicide in young married Traveller men has many impacts, not least the economic difficulties presented for bereaved families in addition to the enormous emotional and psychological effects.

This specific culture-related factor is just one example of the many issues pertinent to the specifics of cause, incidence and profile of suicide within the Traveller community and which require further examination.

RECOMMENDATIONS

1. The active pursuance of a strategy to develop support services specific to Travellers' particular needs should form part of all current mental health programmes and other relevant services. Most importantly, Travellers and other minority communities should be included in targeted groups for specific interventions outlined in the recommendations of the report of *Suicide in Ireland – A National Study 2001*, and the implementation of the following recommendations are particularly relevant to Travellers:

> '...there was another accident and a lot of the same people come, the chief mourning seat is just changed around. It is their time to be in that seat. There is a serious amount of depression after it. It's because of what has happened and it will happen again. You wonder how can that change or what can be done to help the situation.'
>
> Participant,
> Service Provider Focus Group

2. Rec. 3: 'Access to mental health services should be improved by the development of a

community wide flexible range of mental health services. Given the high level of mental illness, barriers to referral or access to mental health services should be eliminated.'

3. Rec. 15: 'Training in suicidal behaviour recognition and management should be available to; community groups, parent associations, youth groups, health care staff, schools, relevant voluntary agencies and professional groups. This training should be adequately resourced and be made available in a systematic and ongoing manner.' (Training should also be designed for people with literacy problems.)

4. Similarly, it is highly appropriate that the recommendations pertaining to mental health contained within *Traveller Health – A National Strategy 2002–2005* should be advanced as soon as possible and specifically the recommendations as follows:

5. Action 82: 'Formal links will be created between community psychiatric services and Traveller organisations in each Health Board area to facilitate early intervention.'

6. Action 83: 'Specific training in Traveller identity and culture will be provided to mental health service providers in order to ensure that such cultural factors are fully understood in meeting the needs of Travellers in this sensitive area.'

7. Action 84: 'The Department of Health and Children will establish a national working group, representing statutory and voluntary mental health service providers, Travellers and Traveller organizations to explore culturally appropriate models of mental health services for Travellers.'

8. While waiting for a full roll-out of the above-mentioned recommendations in every Health Service Executive (HSE) area and in the current absence of suicide prevention measures specific to Travellers, all service providers pertinent to mental health and suicide could work towards reducing barriers in existing counselling and psychiatric services as an immediate measure. This could begin with the implementation of cultural diversity training and the provision of educational information related specifically to Travellers for relevant staff. Liaison with Traveller organisations for expertise, and feedback on issues which might be relevant to providing a more inclusive and needs-specific service, would be a positive asset to such actions.

9. The National Suicide Study found that general practitioners played a pivotal role in suicide prevention and were an important point of contact for those at risk. However, the 1995 UCG/ McCarthy Report found that 17 per cent of Travellers

had difficulty registering with a general practitioner and in many areas only a small number of practitioners provided services to Travellers.[5] Since that time equality legislation and other measures have been introduced to combat practitioner prejudice; however, there has been no follow-up analysis on its effectiveness. What cannot be underestimated is the value of general practitioner support in the process of diagnosis of mental illness, the possible identification of suicidal tendencies and for the onward patient referral to services.

10. Others parties important in the identification of suicidal tendencies and in making onward referrals to services include clergy, public health nurses, chaplains, social workers, family members and friends.

11. It is also especially important that all service providers in contact with Travellers at times of bereavement, especially where related to suicide and where a support need is identified, give advice and/or make a referral to a support service.

CONCLUSIONS

Bringing about a reduction in suicide in Ireland is at critical juncture as identified both in the *Report of the Task Force on Suicide 1998 and Suicide in Ireland – A National Study 2001*, the findings of which contributed to the formulation of a much-needed nationwide prevention strategy launched in September 2005.

A National Traveller Suicide Group was established as a short-term solution to the growing concern of suicide among young Traveller men. Initial funding from the National Office for Suicide Prevention provided for a dedicated suicide worker, awareness raising and the production of appropriate materials. However, while Traveller suicide rates have not been established nationally, the research findings in this book, though specific to some Travellers residing mainly in Dublin, are particularly worrying if they come anywhere close to being representative of the national situation. In fact, since December 2004 (the last date of Parish data analysis) a further eight suicide deaths have occurred.[6]

Clearly, there is a need for *Traveller-specific* suicide data on a national basis, which could

5. *Health Service Provision for the Travelling Community in Ireland, 1995.* Centre for Health Promotion Studies, University College Galway and Patricia McCarthy & Associates, 1995.

6. Six males and two females, of which four occurred in 2005 and four in 2006. The two female deaths are the first and only recorded by the Parish of the Travelling People over the 12-year period.

highlight demographic and cultural risk factors. Without this information developing an all inclusive and effective prevention strategy may be problematic.

There is also a critical need for a long-term prevention campaign specific to Travellers, which takes account of the incidence and risk factors and which dignifies that in a financially commensurate way.

Given that depression presents as the most significant risk factor for suicide, the issue of Travellers' lack of uptake of mental health services has significance. A combined approach based on improving delivery of services in an equitable and culturally appropriate way, and actively targeting Travellers as a specific patient group, could improve their access to mental health and general practitioner services which may in the long term improve suicide prevention.

Chapter 9

Recommendations: The Church and Clergy

A high level of religious observance is common to many Travellers and there is generally a great deal of respect for priests, particularly those who understand Travellers' cultural and religious needs. In contrast, opinions reported at focus groups combined with experiences of staff at the Parish of the Travelling People reveal a reluctance by some clergy to engage with Traveller parishioners, referring their requests for services back to the Parish of the Travelling People. To what degree this prevails is unclear.

It could be said that the existence of a designated parish for Travellers in the Dublin diocese for over 26 years provided a valuable service to its parishioners, however, the services provided were clearly intended to be integrated rather than segregated, adding value to existing church services. For a number of reasons in that time, including ensuring children were receiving a more consistent education, many Travellers adopted a less nomadic lifestyle. As a consequence, many express a greater desire to be included in the activities of the parish they reside in.

> 'Another thing that struck me a few years back was this family, someone died belonging to them and they had to have a Mass every month for a year, and then of course the anniversary.'
>
> *Participant,*
> *Service Provider Focus Group*

CUSTOMS OBSERVED

The language used and customs observed by Travellers at times of death can differ to terms and customs more generally used. For example, Travellers often refer to the 'removal' of the deceased to the church as the 'wake' and some use the term 'Mass' to describe prayers and blessings for the deceased on anniversaries or other occasions. Other examples are the blessing of graves and headstones, pilgrimages to holy places, ninth day and monthly memorial masses, where a mass is held on the corresponding day of the death for 12 months.

> 'When we would be organising the church the first thing the parish priest will say is 'will the priest from the Travelling community be looking after the Mass?' If you say yes, you can sort of feel that his voice changes, he's a very happy man.'
>
> *Participant,*
> *Service Provider Focus Group*

Another possibly unfamiliar custom to some clergy is how people travel very long distances for a funeral and the importance of viewing the body. The combination of these two things can occasionally cause a delay to clerical/ undertaking proceedings, which can lead to frustration.

THE ROLE OF PARISH SISTERS

In the Dublin area, and more specific to accommodation sites, contact between some Traveller families and parish Sisters has been well established, evolving largely through co-operative working projects or through pastoral care and in many cases extending over long periods of time through the course of important life and family occasions.

RECOMMENDATIONS

1. Travellers want good-quality contact with priests at parish level; however, feedback from Travellers and ongoing observations by staff of the Parish of the Travelling People reveal that often clergy and parish personnel are unfamiliar with their Traveller parishioners. Some contrib-uting factors as cited earlier could relate to priests being reluctant to engage with Travellers in their parish. Travellers, on the other hand, though predominantly religious and observant, are not regular Mass attendees, which may also be a limiting factor for contact between both parties.

An issue which could also compound that situation are the changes occurring in the Church in Ireland, resulting in a decline in vocations and which will affect personnel resources at parish level. However, the adoption of creative new approaches catering to all parishioners is most important at a time of decline in faith and followers. In particular, positive actions which aim to target Traveller parishioners specifically, as part of the Church's wide community of followers is critical, and could include the following:

> 'The needs of Travellers are both the same and different to those of any local parish. Some of those needs are steeped in the culture and extraordinary faith of the people, however, as a distinct cultural group one is constantly witnessing issues of discrimination even at times of death. The first blessing everyone receives in Baptism states: "The Christian Community welcomes you with great joy and in its name I claim you for Christ." I question whether the 'Christian Community' does welcome this child who happens to be a Traveller. With regard to the Church institution I think the first response to tragedy ought to be the ability to meet people at a heart and emotional level. I'm reminded of Cardinal Newman's motto cor ad cor loquitur (heart to heart speaks). Empathy/sharing with and being with those who are suffering means that we suffer with them. We then at the appropriate time assist people in every way possible.'
>
> *Fr John Gallagher CM, Parish of the Travelling People (2000–2006)*

2. A call to action to the whole Church via the Bishops Conference to take consideration of the establishment of a national structure, including an Episcopal Promoter (Guideline 89) and National Officer (Guideline 90-91) responsible for the pastoral care of Travellers. Such an office would promote Traveller participation in the life of the Church, guard against discrimination and

> '......because the Travellers have their own parish, it is like 'they aren't our concern, they aren't our problem'. I think a lot of parishes have opted out and not got involved.'
>
> Participant,
> Service Provider Focus Group

develop and deliver cultural awareness training for church communities. These particular offices are outlined in sections 84–99 of *People on the Move: Guidelines for the Pastoral Care of Gypsies* (Pontifical Council for the Pastoral Care of Migrants and Travellers – XXXVIII April 2006).

3. Specifically that the Bishops Conference consider guideline 90 of the *Guidelines* as mentioned above, which recommends the appointment of a national co-ordinator for the pastoral care of Travellers who would engage proactively with priests/religious who are *already* appointed in each diocese to care for the pastoral needs of Travellers.

4. Similarly, it is important for existing parish clergy to identify and engage with Traveller parishioners, establishing contact with families and sites of accommodation.

5. In each diocese a concerted approach to deliver cultural diversity training programmes for clergy, parish councils and other staff within all parishes would be very useful and/or Traveller-specific information related to culture, religious customs and observances to improve knowledge and understanding. Liaison with local and national Traveller organisations in developing this initiative could be beneficial.

> 'If you ask some priests, they would only know one type of Mass and that is in the church. I understand that Mass can be anywhere, it can be Mass in a trailer, it can be Mass anywhere.'
>
> Participant,
> Traveller Focus Group

6. Specifically on issues which may arise for funerals and where for example there is occasionally a delay due to mourners travelling to attend a funeral or view the body of the deceased, it would be helpful if the church or officiating clergy were alerted to this, and important also if the needs being expressed by the bereaved family were respected and accommodated.

7. If all parishioners, including Travellers, recognise and accept the changes taking place in the Church as it responds to ongoing limitations of resources, for example, where services are administered by lay chaplains and parish sisters instead of priests, it will also help meet their demands in the long term.

> 'Some people will have a monument ...... it may be on the road where the accident happened or it may be at the grave. It is a place where the whole family of Travellers meet to pray.'
>
> *Participant, Traveller Focus Group*

8. Bereavement support and counselling services are a very obvious need among many Travellers. Parish Sisters in their pastoral role are frequently involved in supporting families through bereavement and crises, often being the only external witness to a family's or individual's need for support. In that context, it is especially important that where needs being expressed cannot be met by them that they facilitate onward referrals to appropriate services.

CONCLUSION

Religious values are intrinsic to the way of life for many Travellers. However, there is an obvious need for clergy to actively engage with their Traveller parishioners and for training and education to take place in local parishes and amongst clergy generally. More specifically, it is more important than ever for each parish to uphold their responsibility to their Traveller parishioners, as they have become less nomadic and therefore have a greater need to be included in the services of their local parish.

> 'There are some priests out there that I suppose couldn't care less about Travellers as well. They might be a very small number but I know for a fact that the parish where I am I find it very hard to get to know them, even though I see the same priests all the time ...... whether they don't want to get to know the Travellers or whatever.'
>
> *Participant, Traveller Focus Group*

It is imperative that the Church hierarchy in Ireland underpin any strategy to pursue equality and justice for Travellers.

Chapter 10

Recommendations: Funeral Undertakers

Travellers bereaved, like most people, want to avail of a good reliable quality service appropriate to their needs for the burial of their deceased. However, when their needs are not met in an appropriate way, it causes much distress at an already painful time.

In consultation with Travellers regarding the services offered by funeral undertakers, they report mixed levels of satisfaction. High levels of satisfaction were expressed where a service was flexible, responsive to their specific needs and which showed an understanding of issues of cultural importance to them. In turn, Travellers report a loyalty to that service provider by repeat business through families, extended families and friends. However, some Travellers report that they experience a sense of tolerance from some local undertakers, which they regard as preferable to the hostile stance taken by others. As a result, many feel they have little or no choice but to engage with the service that shows tolerance, often returning many times, rather than face rejection or hostility again. Most Travellers discriminated against in these situations do not have the capacity or energy to challenge the discrimination, even after the event, just wanting to get on with their grieving.

While in theory the issue of equality in service provision is enshrined in the equal status legislation, the reality of Travellers' contact with service providers can be quite different, where discrimination still prevails often in covert and subtle ways as demonstrated by indifference and intolerance.

When funeral undertakers are hostile in rural areas, this can be particularly problematic where alternative options are not always available and, not surprisingly, where levels of dissatisfaction are more frequently reported. In response, it is not uncommon for Travellers to feel they have no option

'...the reading and writing is a major problem. They come to us and if they have somebody with them who can sign forms and so on, somebody who would be able to explain in detail to them what you are signing, because they will say they do understand everything and they are only saying it for the sake of saying it and they don't fully understand. If there was something available to them... Every one of us at some time has to arrange funerals. They need a little bit more help.'

Participant,
Service Provider Focus Group

but to secure the services of a Dublin-based funeral undertaker for a rural funeral and burial.

While it is accepted that practices in funeral undertaking vary considerably, some other issues reported by Travellers to be of concern to them included random refusal of services where payment was not made in advance and where personal information regarding funeral arrangements was passed to the Gardaí.

Funeral undertakers, on the other hand, report challenges to service provision as involving delays in services due to altered time schedules for removals and funerals in part due to mourners arriving late and the knock-on effects for other services. Also, the management of large groups of mourners around funeral homes and problems related to literacy difficulties.

RECOMMENDATIONS

1. It is highly recommended that funeral under-takers pursue information to increase their knowledge and understanding of Travellers as a client group, in particular information specific to Travellers' death practices, religious customs and traditions followed.

> 'I have found with the Travelling community that they are very honourable people. Whatever the cost is, it is paid. In the 16 years I haven't had a problem with funerals. The only thing ...... they find it quite difficult to understand the times, what time the removal is, what time the funeral is and so on.'
>
> *Participant,*
> *Service Provider Focus Group*

2. In co-operation with local parishes, funeral undertakers could participate in any specific cultural diversity training programmes being developed (see chapter 9 for recommendations for clergy).

3. For Travellers, providing notice to funeral undertakers of the possibility of late arrivals and the appointment of someone to co-ordinate mourners around the mortuary areas and in hospital car parks, where a large group of people gather, could improve the challenges which sometimes arise.

4. Similarly, funeral undertakers may need to be more flexible to sensitive issues which can occur. One example of this is where there is a possibility of two removals: one in Dublin, the new home of the deceased, and the other in the traditional home and burial ground. Likewise, there may be occasions where there is a need for people who have travelled long distances to be facilitated to view the body outside of the usual times, that is, before or after the funeral Mass.

5. It could be helpful for undertakers to have a consistent strategy to deal with situations where poor literacy may present as an issue. In consultation with the deceased's family, some undertakers consulted found that the family appointing one person to liaise with them in making arrangements, signing forms and linking with the bereaved can be helpful. Another undertaker felt that taking more time with the family, explaining the time schedule and arrangements clearly was useful in preventing potential difficulties or frustrations

6. There has been criticism of some undertakers notifying the Gardaí of Traveller funerals, simply on the basis that there may be conflict, but often without any authentication or consultation with the deceased's family. In the small minority of cases where issues of conflict are genuinely anticipated, it is preferable for undertakers to liaise and consult with the bereaved family first, who are often not involved in the conflict.

CONCLUSION

During a time when Ireland is experiencing unprecedented economic growth and as its culturally diverse population grows, the business sector is continuously reflecting on, and responding to, the changing demands of its wide range of service users. In the funeral undertaking industry there is a certain inevitability of contact with a diverse customer base which places an importance

> 'Both funeral homes I tried for my brother, I had a job getting one. They wouldn't collect the body in Naas. They said 'No sorry we don't do Naas'. I just walked out in temper.'
>
> *Participant,*
> *Service Provider Focus Group*

on understanding issues related to ethnic diversity and sensitivity to customs and rituals practised. A knowledge and understanding of Travellers' cultural needs by funeral undertakers can only lead to improved outcomes for both parties.

Chapter 11

Recommendations:
An Garda Síochána

All service providers in our sample were conscious of the fact that a heavy police presence can cause great distress to Travellers who simply wish to bury their loved ones in peace.

Report on Service Provider Focus Groups
Behaviour & Attitudes Market Research March 2004

Violence and conflict have occurred at a minority of Traveller funerals, causing distress and fear for everyone present, not least the immediate family who frequently have no involvement in the conflict concerned. However, policing Traveller funerals is a contentious issue, creating strong feelings among Travellers, local communities, funeral undertakers, clergy and others. In focus groups conducted with service providers, they expressed mixed views on Garda intervention, citing positive and negative experiences. On the other hand, Travellers perceived Garda intervention as being negative, citing insensitivity in some cases as their main focus for concern.

Some examples highlighted describe an inconsistency in the Gardaí's response where some actions were heavy-handed while others were sensitive. These responses are thought to be influenced not by the situation itself but by the individual Garda involved, and where occasionally these inconsistencies lead to an overzealous approach, for example, in the use of riot gear in anticipation of trouble, causing distress, humiliation and fear for mourners.

Where friction is anticipated at a funeral it is most often Travellers who notify the Gardaí directly or through a priest or funeral director. However, inaccurate reporting by other people is common, causing anxiety and unwarranted stress. This could be avoided by direct liaison with the immediate family, a local priest or community representative in order to substantiate the report.

The Gardaí confirm that the most common reasons for policing Traveller funerals follows a request from a concerned citizen or in some cases a service provider under the Gardaí's remit to protect life or property and keep the peace. They contend also to substantiate any policing requests made to them by contacting the bereaved family concerned. This does not however concur with the experiences of some Travellers and Parish staff who have witnessed on occasions where families were unaware of the Gardaí's intention to be present, until the time of the funeral.

RECOMMENDATIONS

1. There may be exceptional occasions where Garda intervention is required to prevent conflict during a funeral and in these instances consultation with the mourning family is extremely important, not least to establish verification but equally to inform the family, who as previously stated are often uninvolved, and to forge some links with the chief mourners, establishing issues of sensitivity. On the other hand, it is important, where a family are aware of the likelihood of conflict, to report such concerns to the Gardaí for the protection of all mourners.

2. Where policing occurs at a funeral, demonstrating respect and sensitivity is fundamentally important. Examples of insensitivity cited include occasions where there was excessive use of riot gear, establishing checkpoints to examine vehicle tax and insurance, searching cars, corralling mourners around graves and walking and standing on graves, resulting in understandable resentment and anger. The consistent and comprehensive adoption of the policies of the Garda Racial and Intercultural Unit, especially in relation to searching and riot gear, would greatly help to avoid unnecessary distress at funerals.

3. Where verification of a request for policing is proving difficult, it could be helpful if the Garda involved made contact with the local Garda community liaison officer and other community representatives, including priests who could assist and provide intervention and liaison with the mourning family.

4. On other occasions where there is likely to be a very large attendance of mourners, which is not uncommon, it would be helpful that Travellers notify the Gardaí for traffic control purposes.

CONCLUSION

Violence at Traveller funerals has occurred in a small minority of cases and often amongst a small minority of mourners. Nonetheless, the conflict and the policing tactics deployed have an impact on all mourners. Balancing the protection of life and property while exercising sensitivity during these emotional occasions has created challenges and significant problems in relations between the Gardaí and Travellers, which needs to be addressed.

'I couldn't understand it. It was an ordinary family funeral. And when you looked around the graveyard there were Gardaí everywhere and it took the whole family feel out of that funeral. It was horrendous.'

Participant,
Service Provider Focus Group

Similarly, addressing inconsistencies related to verification procedures, methods and styles of policing adopted and the lack of liaison with Traveller families is also vital to improving contact between both parties.

Chapter 12

Recommendations: The Prison Service

No figures are available for the number of Travellers in prisons, as figures compiled by the Irish Prison Service identify prisoners by nationality and not by ethnic identity.

For any prisoner, the death of a loved one while in prison is particularly harrowing, reinforcing their sense of isolation from family. Therefore, providing support to bereaved prisoners is vital. However, bereavement counselling is not currently available in prisons and chaplains are relied upon to respond to the support needs of prisoners at those times. Also in this context, there are no policies, guidelines or basic information for staff, including chaplains, on issues of cultural relevance to prisoners of minority communities, such as Travellers, during times of death.

In the wider context of diversity policy and training, the Prison Service report that policies are being evaluated to address broader elements of anti-racism and interculturalism. Currently, only basic cultural diversity training is provided for prison staff but not for chaplains. They contend that chaplains are responsible for their own training; however, all prison chaplains, while nominated by the Diocesan Bishops, are employed directly by the Department of Justice. Furthermore, chaplains report that they do not provide training in cultural diversity but rely instead on an individual chaplain's experience of pastoral care combined with any previous training or awareness of anti-racism and interculturalism. The Irish Prison Chaplaincy Service comprises 20 full-time and three part-time chaplains, including ordained priests, non-ordained religious and five lay people.

The family both immediate and extended is central to Traveller culture. Similarly, central in the death context is respecting and honouring the dead and participating in the traditions practised around those times. For Traveller prisoners to be isolated from their family in the event of a death is very difficult, especially where they are unable to attend funeral services. However, the current policy on compassionate temporary release only occasionally permits release to prisoners, leading to hurt and anger.

Recommendations

1. The development of a comprehensive intercultural prison service training programme for all prison staff, including chaplains, is important to Traveller prisoners in their contact with staff, in this case, at times of death and bereavement. The current training policy, which excludes chaplains, clearly requires some consideration by all parties, that is, the Prison Service, the Department of Justice, Diocesan Bishops, and the Chaplaincy Service, and it seems prudent that chaplains should be included in any proposed training strategies being currently considered by the Irish Prison Service. In the meantime, the Chaplaincy Service should be facilitated to provide their own induction and in-service intercultural training.

2. Specific information based on Traveller culture and death-related customs and observances would be helpful for all staff, improving knowledge and understanding. Liaison with local and national Traveller organisations in compiling such information could be beneficial.

> 'They can't grieve. The natural thing is they want to be with their family when their sister or brother dies. Sometimes they do get out but a lot of the time they don't. It does cause an awful lot of frustration.'
>
> *Participant,*
> *Service Provider Focus Group*

3. The appointment of specific cultural liaison staff would be a positive asset to prison services, in catering to a diverse prison population, including Travellers, and who could provide specific support during critical times such as death and bereavement.

4. There is a very definite need for structured bereavement services to be made available to all prisoners, including Travellers. In the meantime where chaplains are unable to meet specific support needs, they are integral to commissioning services from outside sources.

5. The impact of the death of a family member is very difficult for prisoners and to be denied release to attend mortuary or funeral services is particularly hard. The effect of this on prisoners has concerned prison chaplains for some time, and as a result they made recommendations to the Department of Justice in 2004 and 2005 on the issue of compassionate temporary release. To date no action has been taken. They recommended as follows:

   National Prison Chaplains' Annual Report 2004: 'Family bereavement has been a concern for the Chaplains in the Irish Prison Service for some time, and has been highlighted in previous reports. For a prisoner, bereavement is particularly traumatic and devastating. Incarceration isolates individuals from their families. At a time of bereavement, therefore, it is particularly important that they are reunited with their families to be allowed grieve and mutually support each other. This will help diffuse the anger and resentment that we meet in our work, where prisoners have been refused to attend the funeral of an immediate family member.'

National Prison Chaplains' Annual Report 2005: 'We recommended in last year's report that it be accepted as the norm that all prisoners would be allowed to attend the funeral of close family members. We welcome some improvement in this area and urge that there would be a sustained move towards greater compassion in the decision making around temporary release for sentenced prisoners.'

6. In the meantime, where release is denied on the death of a family member, developing a policy across all prisons to mark the occasion of a death could be helpful to Traveller and other prisoners in order to empower them to feel participative in honouring their deceased.

7. As there is a custom of common names within Traveller families, it is important that prisons clarify details of the deceased before a prisoner is informed. It has been reported by Travellers that occasionally errors in the notification of the death of a loved one, for example, where the news of the death of a brother instead of correctly an uncle or father has led to great upset.

Conclusion

The scope for developing a much-needed broader diversity policy, catering to Traveller prisoners as a specific group, is very timely to strategies being currently considered by the Prison Service. The fact that no formal intercultural training or awareness programmes are offered to prison chaplains by any of the interested parties, that is, the Prison Service via the Department of Justice as their employer and Diocesan Bishops as their nominators, or that there are no bereavement counselling services available within prisons requires considerable re-evaluation.

SECTION 4

QUALITATIVE RESEARCH

Chapter 13

Reports of Focus Groups

TRAVELLERS AND SERVICE PROVIDERS

Research was commissioned for the purpose of this book to establish key factors related to the experiences of Travellers and service providers in contact with Travellers at times of death. Specifically, two focus groups were held which sought to establish relevant issues pertaining to the interaction between both groups and to examine the barriers affecting Travellers' engagement with services. The findings provided a firmer foundation from which to look at those issues in more detail and to explore steps to provide solutions to them.

Research focus groups were conducted in March and May 2004 and comprised:

> ➢ Travellers
> ➢ Priests
> ➢ Hospital and prison chaplains
> ➢ Hospital and local health nurses
> ➢ Social workers
> ➢ Undertaker
> ➢ Gardaí.

A. Traveller Workshop

Introduction

■ This report presents the findings of a small scale pilot study carried out among Travellers by Behaviour & Attitudes during March 2004.

■ The objective of the pilot study was to explore Traveller perceptions of certain aspects of their culture relating to sickness, hospitalisation, death, burial and mourning.

■ The objective was to provide some understanding of how beliefs and attitudes in relation to these topics influence behaviour patterns at times of hospitalisation, extended illness, death in the family, burial and so on.

■ It was been evident for some time that some Traveller customs in these areas can lead to misunderstandings with relevant service providers who, for the most part, are from the settled community and who, as a consequence, may find some of the practices difficult to understand.

■ This, in turn, can lead to points of friction.

■ The pilot study took the form of one group discussion with selected Travellers. The group discussion was conducted on March 23rd in the Traveller's Parish Centre in Phibsboro.

■ This summary document will be distributed to a small group of people who come into contact with the Traveller community at some of the stress points considered here. The intention is that these notes may serve as a sort of briefing document for a group discussion among these "service providers". The hope for that group discussion (which is scheduled to take place on the 7th of April) is that we may resolve:

 □ To what extent service providers are already aware of the factors influencing Traveller practice and behaviour in these areas.

 □ To explore the extent to which the practices exercised by Travellers can lead to a breakdown in understanding or a potential problem for service providers.

 □ To explore what possibilities may exist for resolving some of the conflict areas while recognising the sensitivities involved on both sides.

■ In the pages which follow we attempt to summarise the key indicators from the initial group discussion. Given the small scale nature of the study, it would, of course, be unrealistic to assume that we might capture the full range of cultural factors operating in this highly sensitive area. Our hope is that the points which follow will serve as a useful agenda for Phase 2 of the study.

NOTE ON REPORT STRUCTURE

- The structure we have adopted for this summary is as follows:
  - ➤ Key formative experiences
  - ➤ Some notes on the Traveller "mindset", as they emerged in this review
  - ➤ Key issues in relation to illness and hospitalisation
  - ➤ Death and mourning
  - ➤ Burial arrangements

- The report concludes with some incidental issues which arose in the course of the project.

THE TRAVELLER EXPERIENCE

- In presenting this summary we are highly conscious of the fact that the indicators are based on a very small sample of respondents and ones with a degree of attachment to the Parish.

- This may mean that their own behaviour patterns are not completely representative of the patterns among a wider cross-section of Travellers. We attempted to overcome this difficulty, as best we could, by asking people to describe not just their own behaviour patterns but those of other members of the Traveller community.

- There seemed to be a number of common formative experiences which have a bearing on Traveller mindsets as we will attempt to describe later:
  - ☐ Most Travellers tend to be from larger family units than the contemporary average.
  - ☐ There seems to be a considerable level of contact with extended family groups: more so than would be the norm in the settled community.

- On the basis of the experiences reported by this small group, Travellers seem to have higher than average incidences of:
  - ☐ Child mortality

- ☐ Accidents of various kinds (car accidents, fires, etc.)

- ☐ Death among young adults (including suicides)

- ☐ Confrontations with police authorities

  - Quite often triggered by a sense (on the part of Travellers) of being discriminated against

- Although firm figures from published sources are not readily available, the general indicators tend to confirm this pattern of disadvantage.

- Disappointingly the most recent Traveller health and mortality figures available are those of the 1986 Economic, Social and Research Institute Report and record:

  - ☐ Traveller infant mortality is 2.5 times greater than the national average.

  - ☐ Settled men have a life expectancy of 75 years – Traveller men have a life expectancy of 65 years. *(HRB '87)*

  - ☐ Settled women have a life expectancy of 78 years – Traveller women have a life expectancy of 65 years. *(HRB '87)*

  - ☐ Travellers have higher death rates for all causes of death among the settled community. *(HRB '87)*

  - ☐ In a 5 year period, for every settled child that died of a cot death 10 Traveller children died of a cot death. *(Irish Sudden Infant Death Association)*

  - ☐ Travellers over 65 years account for only 3.3% of the Traveller population compared with 11.1% of the general population. *(Census 2002)*

- Childhood memories of school days quite often focus on instances of being treated differently (picked out for separate treatment and discriminated against).

- On the basis of this small sample, Travellers seem to move relatively freely between Ireland and the UK:

  - ☐ These experience can sometimes lead to comparisons between service facilities in the two states (a point we return to later).

THE TRAVELLER MINDSET

- Family matters are of key importance. That is, of course, true of all cultures. The distinctive feature evident here however seems to be in the definition of family.

- The extended family seems to have a high importance in the Traveller mindset.

- There seems to be a high regard for people providing a service or function and particularly in this instance for

  - The priest

  - The doctor

- Travellers can be disappointed to perhaps a surprising degree (from the perspective of outsiders), if these authority figures do not live up to Traveller expectations.

- There is a high degree of religious fervour evident, of a type that is quite rare nowadays in the settled community.

- Thus, there is a strong commitment to formal religion and to contact with priests and nuns.

- Alongside that, however, there is an equally fervent belief in mystical individuals, faith healers, holy places, relics, etc.

- There is a palpable fear of serious illness, hospitalisation and death.

- There is a strong commitment to prayer, sacrifice, fasting, etc. as a basis for gaining favour and delivery from "harm".

- Attitudes towards illness and death seem to be so deep-seated among Travellers as to evoke a strong belief in, and commitment to, prayer and comfort for the sick or the bereaved and intervention on behalf of those who have died, in the form of masses and memorial services.

- This sense of needing to show one's commitment to the dead combines with feelings of family solidarity and a fear of being discriminated against to evoke certain beliefs and behaviour patterns in regard to the lavishness of funeral arrangements, the choice of headstones and graveyard memorials.

ILLNESS AND HOSPITALISATION

- The mindset described in the preceding sections results in a situation where certain responses to illness and hospitalisation are considered the norm.

  - Traveller experience with high levels of mortality mean that illness and hospitalisation is taken very seriously.

  - The strong emphasis on community support means that people place a high value on visiting and offering support to anybody who is ill.

  - The emphasis on family responsibilities in this area are such that people feel they would be letting themselves and the family down by failing to appear sufficiently concerned about the problem.

- ☐ Strong adherence to group norms means that Travellers tend to turn up as a group to "pay their respects".

- ☐ They recognise that this can cause significant problems for hospital staff but the importance of their beliefs, customs and practices seems to override all.

- ☐ In these circumstances Travellers clearly feel that there is little wrong with camping in hospital compounds to be close to their loved ones.

- There is an extreme fear that things will go wrong. Linked to this there is a need to be on hand immediately so that the person who is unwell is "among their own" and has the opportunity to pass on any "last wishes" – something which Travellers place a great deal of store in.

- We encountered some reports of cases where Travellers had visited sick relatives in hospitals in the UK where special arrangements were made, by the hospital authorities, to allow them stay over extended periods (with appropriate accommodation, wash-up facilities, etc.).

- ☐ This leads to expectations that similar facilities will be available in Ireland.

DEATH AND MOURNING

- It is very clear from the stories surrounding incidents of death and mourning that this kind of behaviour can lead to conflict with hospital authorities.

- The problem can become compounded when Travellers see authority figures (of whom they have very high expectations) behaving in a manner which they feel is insensitive to their needs.

- In these circumstances the position is not helped by the sense of feeling isolated or discriminated against. There were a number of reports of Travellers feeling that they were:

- ☐ Talked down to by hospital staff or

- ☐ They felt that hospital staff were talking about them in a critical manner, out of earshot.

- As would have been evident from an earlier section of the report, Travellers seem to have a very highly developed sense of the fear of death.

- Travellers seem to place great store in being surrounded by their loved ones at a time of death: accompanying the dying person on their journey, so to speak.

- There is a marked sense of a need to mark the deceased's passing and to make strong religious intercession on that person's behalf.

- In part this seems to be related to a sense of how important it is to show how much one loved and misses the deceased.

- Different rituals seem to be evoked by different family groupings towards the end of life.

- Most seem to have a special arrangement for blessing the person's grave.

- Some have a special service nine days after burial.

- Others have a mass at monthly intervals for the 12 month period after the burial.

- Others are reducing the frequency of such services to once a quarter or once every six months.

- Not all priests seem to be aware of these customs and Travellers clearly attach special significance to priests who make an effort to be in attendance when somebody is gravely ill or immediately after they have died. Similarly, they expect priests to understand their rituals in regard to when and how often they will have memorial services.

BURIAL

- It seems clear that they have a very strong compunction to spend as much as possible on all such demonstrations of loss and devotion.

- There is a palpable fear by some that to do any less would be interpreted by extended family members in a bad light.

- The choice of funeral arrangement, burial ground, coffin or casket and headstone are all elements of special significance to Travellers.

- We encountered in a number of instances issues related to :

  - Where a person should be buried, whether in a traditional or new burial ground

  - Whether in a casket or a coffin

- Issues of these kind are given such an important ranking that Travellers are clearly willing to put themselves in debt to meet what they see as their responsibilities in this area.

- Some undertakers clearly have a high degree of familiarity with Traveller funerals and have established a strong working relationship with the Traveller community.

- Others can cause considerable offence by (for example) demanding payment in advance for particular types of services or making Travellers feel unwelcome.

INCIDENTIAL ISSUES

- The main focus of the discussion was on matters relating to illness and death.

- Inevitably however a number of other issues were raised in relation to Traveller contacts with service providers of various kinds.

- It seems clear that the Traveller community has a very tense relationship with the Gardaí.

- Travellers recognise that some members of their community behave in a manner which can lead to problems:

  □ Nevertheless, it can be very upsetting to have, what is deemed to be, inappropriate police intervention directed at mourners in funeral corteges.

- There are also incidental problems that can arise in dealings with hospital staff, prison wardens, social workers and school teachers but these can perhaps be discussed in greater detail in the second phase of the project.

B. SERVICE PROVIDER WORKSHOP

INTRODUCTION

→ This report presents the findings from the second phase of a small scale pilot study carried out by Behaviour & Attitudes during May 2004.

→ An earlier phase of the pilot study consisted of a group discussion with members of the Traveller community discussing Traveller perceptions of certain aspects of their culture relating to sickness, hospitalisation, death, burial and mourning.

→ The second group discussion examined these issues from the perspective of people in the settled community who provide relevant services to Travellers.

   ■ Respondents in this second group discussion included priests (including hospital and prison chaplains) hospital and local health nurses, social workers, an undertaker and a member of the Gardaí. All had a number of years direct experience of working with Travellers.

→ The objective of this phase of the research was to explore:

   ■ The extent to which members of this informed group had developed an understanding of the specific needs of Travellers in the key areas under consideration.

   ■ To what extent they feel current services are adequate to meet demands in the area.

   ■ What suggestions they might have for improving matters.

→ It must be stressed that the sample size for the project is extremely small. The results must therefore be viewed as broadly indicative rather than definitive.

→ Given the scale of the project, the findings are presented in summary format only.

SUMMARY OF KEY PROBLEM AREAS

→ The first point to make is that people in this target audience clearly think deeply about the problems confronted by Travellers in Irish society.

→ Almost all laid emphasis on the fact that it had taken them some considerable time to develop an understanding of Traveller culture.

→ In almost all cases, that understanding had been developed by the individuals concerned without any significant assistance from other sources, manuals or advisory texts.

→ The second clear finding from this brief study is that expert observers (as represented by our group respondents) are highly conscious that Travellers do have specific problems which arise in the context of sickness, hospitalisation, death, burial and mourning.

→ These derive from a combination of factors:

■ A perceived high incidence of certain illnesses among Travellers, significantly higher than the national average.

■ A set of cultural norms existing among Travellers which produces certain patterns of behaviour which are, in turn, different from those of settled people.

■ An absence of awareness or understanding of the basis of these differences among the broader mass of service providers in the relevant areas.

→ The recent arrival of large numbers of immigrants with distinctive cultural differences has served to focus attention on the fact that no specific allowances are made for the Traveller community as one with separate cultural needs. As one respondent expressed it:

■ *"It is even more the case now with our non-national community. I'm sure it is probably the same in every hospital, but I know that we at St. James, we recently appointed a cultural diversity officer for our non-nationals whereby we have a folder on cultural diversity. I picked it up last night to have a look at it and it has every culture and religion and their beliefs, their needs and what have you set out. Our Travelling community are not set down as a separate culture".*

The Traveller Community – Differential Levels Of Illness

→ The strong belief among this target audience is that Travellers have significantly higher levels of health problems.

→ The general belief, which is supported by findings confirmed in the report of the Traveller Workshop, is that Travellers have higher instances of:

■ Child mortality

- Deaths among young people from a combination of illnesses, accidents or suicides.

- Heart disease

- Diabetes

- Depression

→ The belief is that many of these problems are the result of poor housing and lifestyle considerations.

→ Among this group the prevailing view is that not enough has been done to improve the living conditions of Travellers.

→ There is feeling that, among the settled community at large, there is a tendency to blame Travellers for the shortcomings in their living conditions. Among this target group however there is a feeling that living conditions could be improved significantly with appropriate action from the authorities:

- It is felt that there are certain exemplary accommodation sites where living conditions for Travellers are significantly enhanced and the health records show the benefits of this.

- The problem is that there are too few such well planned and serviced sites.

THE IMPACT OF CULTURAL NORMS

→ There is widespread recognition among this target audience that certain aspects of Traveller culture can lead to misunderstandings and difficulties in liaison with the settled community.

- Firstly, there are certain aspects of Traveller culture which, it is acknowledged, can lead to difficulties in liaison with health workers, undertakers, the Gardaí and so on.

- One key difficulty arises from the complex set of Traveller attitudes towards illness and in particular illness that involves hospitalisation.

- Secondly, allied to this there is a very strong commitment to family solidarity and support.

- Thirdly, levels of literacy in the Traveller community are significantly lower than average and this can lead to some misunderstandings.

- This can also lead to higher levels of problems with medical instructions, for example, which can often be seen as confusing by Travellers.

- A further issue which can lead to problems is that of Travellers being less attuned to issues of strict timekeeping and in regard to rules generally.

→ Perhaps the most important cultural difference which can give rise to problems is that of differences in Traveller perceptions of the efficacy of different types of health treatment. Among the Traveller community, there is a high level of belief in healers and healing. There is perhaps rather less understanding of, and commitment, to more conventional healing methods.

→ A combination of these various factors can lead to problems which are familiar and well attested.

- Travellers will wish to turn up in very large numbers to visit hospitalised individuals and also to attend funerals.

- This can lead to significant problems for hospital staff and, sometimes, for undertakers, Gardaí and so on.

- Very firmly indented beliefs in healers, outside conventional medical services, can lead to a situation where even patients who are seriously ill with be reluctant to go to hospital, reluctant to stay there. Because of fear of hospitals, Travellers may leave things so late as to be a danger to the individual concerned.

- This can cause significant anxiety for health workers who have a strong commitment to conventional health methods and a fear that Travellers are prone to be taken advantage of by "Quacks".

- Low levels of literacy and problems experienced with technical language or instructions and with disregard for appointments of various kinds can, inevitably, lead to tensions and difficulties.

- The most severe cases can arise at funerals. This presents the Gardaí with a particular dilemma. They are caught between coping with the demands of the settled community to maintain order on the one hand while allowing Travellers the freedom to bury their dead relatives in a manner that is consonant with their cultural norms.

- It is freely acknowledged that significant problems have arisen in this area with violence erupting at Traveller funerals.

→ On the other hand, all of the service providers in our sample were conscious of the fact that a heavy police presence can cause great distress to Travellers who simply wish to bury their loved ones in peace.

POSSIBLE SOLUTIONS

→ The consensus view among this target audience is that solutions to the problems that arise are not going to be easy to find.

→ The people in this target audience are torn between their wishes to recognise and respond to Traveller culture on the one hand a wish to encourage Travellers to adapt to settled culture on the other.

→ One aspect of this is the confusion that people sometimes feel about the optimum development path for the future. Is it better for Travellers to maintain a distance from the settled community or are they better serviced by integrating more into the cultural norms of their settled neighbours?

→ A sub-division of this general concern is the issue of whether it is better to have specialist services for Travellers or not. It is felt, for example, that having a separate Travellers' Parish can be helpful in certain circumstances in catering for people's religious needs. At the same time, people fear that having such a differentiated service can lead to other service providers feeling that they have no roles or responsibilities in this area.

→ In general the feeling is that there has been too little attention given to making service providers at all levels aware of the different culture needs of Travellers so that problem areas can be anticipated and, where possible, remedied.

→ These experienced service providers feel that they are very much in a minority and rather isolated.

→ That sense is evident in relation to all areas of service provision touched upon by our sample. It is felt however that there are particular problems in relation to dealings with the Gardaí. Such dealings almost always begin at a disadvantage because of the inevitably fraught nature of many of the points of contact.

→ One final point of agreement is that, given the paucity of resources assigned to the

area at present, there is a strong need for cooperation among those groups who currently have some degree of commitment to the problems confronting Travellers. As one respondent put it:

- "I firmly believe that until we all start working under a joint body and we are all saying the same messages with the Travellers on board as well, I feel the statutory authorities, the voluntarily bodies, the Travellers themselves, the community development groups that are working with the Travellers, that we work as a group and carry it forward. That is a short-term plan I know but … "

→ In this regard, there is a sense among service providers (and this view was shared by Travellers themselves) that service provisions for Travellers in the UK are often better than those that would be available in Ireland. It was felt that this applied to housing, hospital arrangements and involvement in the educational system. Clearly this is an issue that would need to be checked more thoroughly but, if it is true, then it may be worth exploring what lessons can be learned from a comparison between how our two societies have handled these issues.

Appendix I
Traveller Mortality Tables

TABLE A1: MALE TRAVELLER MORTALITY RATES

Cause	Gender	2–14 yrs	15–24 yrs	25–39 yrs	40–59 yrs	60–74 yrs	75 yrs+	Total
Coronary	Male	0	1	3	8	11	4	**27**
Stroke	Male	0	0	0	2	3	4	**9**
Road traffic accidents	Male	2	14	8	5	2	0	**31**
Cancer	Male	2	1	1	3	6	0	**13**
Alcohol	Male	0	0	6	1	2	0	**9**
Drugs	Male	0	6	6	0	0	0	**12**
Violent	Male	0	3	2	2	0	0	**7**
Accidental	Male	0	2	4	3	0	0	**9**
Suicide	Male	0	4	11	3	0	0	**18**
Genetic	Male	3	1	0	0	0	0	**4**
All other causes	Male	0	1	0	0	4	0	**5**
Totals		7	33	41	27	28	8	**144**
Actual numbers: The total sample of all males 2 years and over								

TABLE A2: FEMALE TRAVELLER MORTALITY RATES

Cause	Gender	2–14 yrs	15–24 yrs	25–39 yrs	40–59 yrs	60–74 yrs	75 yrs+	Total
Coronary	Female	0	0	1	0	2	5	8
Stroke	Female	0	0	1	0	3	0	4
Road traffic accidents	Female	1	0	0	0	1	0	2
Cancer	Female	0	0	3	10	3	0	16
Alcohol	Female	0	0	1	4	0	0	5
Drugs	Female	0	1	0	0	0	0	1
Violent	Female	0	0	1	0	0	0	1
Accidental	Female	1	0	2	2	0	0	5
Suicide	Female	0	0	0	0	0	0	0
Genetic	Female	4	1	1	0	0	0	6
All other causes	Female	2	0	1	1	5	6	15
Totals		8	2	11	17	14	11	63
Actual numbers: The total sample of all females 2 years and over								

Cause	Gender	2–14 yrs	15–24 yrs	25–39 yrs	40–59 yrs	60–74 yrs	75 yrs+	Total
Coronary	Female	0	0	1	0	2	5	35
	Male	0	1	3	8	11	4	
Stroke	Female	0	0	1	0	3	0	13
	Male	0	0	0	2	3	4	
Road traffic accidents	Female	1	0	0	0	1	0	33
	Male	2	14	8	5	2	0	
Cancer	Female	0	0	3	10	3	0	29
	Male	2	1	1	3	6	0	
Alcohol	Female	0	0	1	4	0	0	14
	Male	0	0	6	1	2	0	
Drugs	Female	0	1	0	0	0	0	13
	Male	0	6	6	0	0	0	
Violent	Female	0	0	1	0	0	0	8
	Male	0	3	2	2	0	0	
Accidental	Female	1	0	2	2	0	0	14
	Male	0	2	4	3	0	0	
Suicide	Female	0	0	0	0	0	0	18
	Male	0	4	11	3	0	0	
Genetic	Female	4	1	1	0	0	0	10
	Male	3	1	0	0	0	0	
All other causes	Female	2	0	1	1	5	6	20
	Male	0	1	0	0	4	0	
Totals		15	35	52	44	42	19	207

Actual numbers: The total sample of all people 2 years and over

Appendix II
Useful Contacts

DEPRESSION SUPPORT

AWARE
72 Lower Leeson Street
Dublin 2
Tel: 01 6617 211
Locall: 1890 303302
Website: www.iol.ie/aware
Email: aware@iol.ie

SUICIDE SUPPORT

Traveller Suicide Prevention Officer
c/o 6 New Cabra Road
Phibsborough
Dublin 7
Tel: 01 8388 874

National Office for Suicide Prevention
Health Service Executive
Dr Steeven's Hospital
Dublin 8
Tel: 01 635 2139 / 635 2179
Website: www.nosp.ie
Email: info@nosp.ie

Bereaved by Suicide Foundation (Console)
All Hallows College
Grace Park Road
Drumcondra
Dublin 9
Tel: 1800 201 890
Website www.suicidebereaved.com
Email: info@console.ie
Meeting: first Monday of month
Contact: Ciara O Connor

Sólás
Barnardos
Christchurch Square
Dublin 8
Tel: 01 4732110
Email: solas@barnardos.ie

Irish Association of Suicidology
16 New Antrim Street
Castlebar
Mayo
Tel: 094 9250 858
Website: www.ias.ie
Email: office@ias.ie

National Suicide Bereavement Support Network
PO Box 1
Youghal
Cork
Website: www.nsbsn.org
Email: info@nsbsn.org

Samaritans
112 Marlborough Street
Dublin 1
Tel: 1850 609 090
Website: www.samaritans.org

BEREAVEMENT SUPPORT

Rainbows Ireland Ltd
National Office
Loreto Centre
Crumlin Road
Dublin 12
Tel: 01 4734 175
Email: rainbows@eircom.net

The Miscarriage Association of Ireland
Carmichael Centre
North Brunswick Street
Dublin 7
Tel: 01 8735 702 / 01 8725 550
Website: www.coombe.ie

Irish Hospice Foundation
4th Floor
Morrison Chambers
32 Nassau Street
Dublin 2
Tel: 01 6793188
Website: www.hospice-foundation.ie
Email: info@hospice-foundation.ie

National Association of Widowers and Deserted Husbands Association
54 Foster Terrace
Ballybough
Dublin 3
Tel: 01 8552 334

Irish Sudden Infant Death Association
Carmichael House
4 North Brunswick Street
Dublin 7
Tel: 01 873 2711
Support helpline: 1850 391 391
Website: www.iol.ie/~isidansr
Email: isida@gofree.indigo.ie

TRAVELLER ORGANISATIONS

Irish Traveller Movement
4/5 Eustace Street
Dublin 2
Tel: 01 679 6577
Web: www.itmtrav.ie
Email: itmtrav@indigo.ie

Exchange House Travellers Service
61 Great Strand Street
Dublin 1
Tel: 01 872 1094
Website: www.exchangehouse.ie
Email: info@exchangehouse.ie

Pavee Point
46 North Great Charles Street
Dublin 1
Tel: 01 878 0255
Website: www.paveepoint.ie
Email: pavee@iol.ie

Parish of the Travelling People
St Laurence House
6 New Cabra Road
Phibsborough
Dublin 7
Tel: 01 8388 874
www.stpetersphibsboro.ie/Travellers.htm
Email: mail@ptrav.ie